ROAD TO REMBETIKA

ROAD TO REMBETIKA

music of a Greek sub-culture
songs of love, sorrow and hashish

BY

GAIL HOLST

DENISE HARVEY (PUBLISHER) · LIMNI, EVIA, GREECE

Published by Denise Harvey (Publisher), 340 05 Limni, Evia, Greece

Cover design: Dimitris Arvanitis
Old photographs were lent
by Kostas Hadzidoulis and Ilias Petropoulos.
Most of the other photographs
were taken with loving care by Eugene Vanderpool.

Road to Rembetika
is the eleventh publication in
THE ROMIOSYNI SERIES

The books published in the Romiosyni Series are concerned with the
forms and expressions of Greek life and culture that emerged during
the post-Byzantine period while still remaining deeply rooted in what
is often referred to as the 'Greek East'. This life and culture is often
identified by the enigmatic word *Romiosyni*, which derives from the
connection of the Greeks with 'new Rome' — Constantinople — and
the Eastern Roman Empire. People who dwelt within this Empire
called themselves *Romioi* — Romans — hence *Romiosyni*, which in a
non-nationalistic sense could be rendered as Hellenism.
Romiosyni is a word that has both historical and emotional
connotations and expresses for the modern Greek a particular aspect
of his national identity. Historically, this identity was not limited to a
political, racial or territorial boundary, and this sense of nationality
depended more on the sharing of a certain milieu, almost a state of
mind, than on anything else.

For more information about these books, please visit
www.deniseharveypublisher.gr

ISBN 978-960-7120-07-6

Για όλους τους ρεμπέτες του ντουνιά
and for my father
who was one of them

Contents

A rembetis: 'The Teacher'.

Preface to the fourth edition

A long time has passed since I wrote this small book as an introduction to the songs known as the rembetika, also spelt rebetika. Despite the fact that it was produced by what was then a tiny publishing house in Athens, with virtually no overseas distribution, the book seemed to find its way into the hands of many people who were interested in Greece and Greek music. During the years since 1975, the rembetika have been the subject of considerable popular and scholarly interest. Books, articles and academic papers have been written about the music, hundreds, perhaps thousands of recordings and re-recordings of the songs have been made, films have been shot, broadcasts made, ensembles formed to play the music in Europe, the United States and Australia.

It is always embarrassing to re-read one's work, especially when it was written thirty years ago. I have tried to correct the most obvious mistakes in the text, and to make some changes in my translations, but not to re-write the book. What I have written subsequently on the rembetika is included in the bibliography together with a selection of articles and books that readers may find useful. Research into the rembetika is still hampered by the lack of reliable sources. This is true of most areas of popular culture in Greece and the late Ottoman Empire, and encourages researchers to speculate or focus on the hard evidence we have: the recordings themselves, record catalogues, photographs, literary descriptions. Unfortunately, recordings are made for a market that already exists and do not represent the original context of the music, and there are only a small number of interviews and autobiographies of rembetika musicians and I regret not having interviewed more musicians when I had the opportunity.

Few subjects have aroused such controversy in Greek cultural life as the rembetika songs. In the Greek translation of this book, we included a series of articles from Greek newspapers and journals of the immediate post-war period that dealt with the rembetika.[1] Played out largely in the pages of the journal *Epitheorisi Technis* (*Arts Review*) and in the Leftist newspapers *Avghi* (*Dawn*) and *Rizospastis* (*Radicalist*), the debate about the rembetika was long and passionate. The music was viewed by many in bourgeois Greek society as 'oriental' and outmoded, a relic from the Ottoman period with which many modern Greeks wished to sever all ties. For Leftwing intellectuals there were serious questions about the moral content of the songs and their effect on the morale of the working-classes. The musicologist Vassilis Papadimitriou, to take one example, claimed the songs eroded popular music and 'spiritually and psychologically polluted the people'.[2] Other Leftist critics claimed the rembetika as the expression of a marginalized working-class during the inter-war period (Holst, *Δρόμος,* pp. 231–7). Composer Mikis Theodorakis was accused of sacrilege by Leftist intellectuals for setting the poetry of major Greek poets such as Yiannis Ritsos to music using elements of rembetika music; still worse, in the eyes of such critics, was his use of the bouzouki and a rembetika singer to interpret his music. His fellow-composer, Manos Hadzidakis, had been the first intellectual to champion the rembetika in a speech he gave at the Arts Theatre of Greece in 1949. He passionately defended the beauty of the whole phenomenon of the rembetika: the lyrics, the music and the dance (see Holst, *Δρόμος,* pp. 151–5). Both composers saw themselves as taking the rembetika to a new plane of sophistication.

If we could summarize the conflict about the rembetika, we would have to say that like many other phenomena in this small and proud nation, the songs were admired to the extent that they were seen as Greek, and despised when considered foreign. References to drugs and the underworld were viewed by the opponents of the rembetika as part of the Ottoman legacy, but few critics knew or cared that many

---

[1] The selection of articles was made largely by Yiannis Kondoyiannis, to whom I am most grateful.

[2] See Holst, *Δρόμος γιά τό Ρεμπέτικο*, Athens: Denise Harvey, 1977, pp. 145–51.

of the songs were simply Turkish tunes with Greek words.[1] Despite the fact that quite a number of the songs written by Vassilis Tsitsanis dealt with the world of the hashish-smoking rembetes, he was credited, by some, for having rescued the songs from the depraved milieu of the hashish dens and brought them into the true province of the Greek soul (Christianopoulos, 1961).[2] As their elements were incorporated into the music of middle-class composers, some Greeks lamented the gentrification of the rembetika and their once colourful, if sordid, environs. One such afficionado was Ilias Petropoulos, whose *Rembetika Traghoudia* (*Ρεμπέτικα Τραγούδια*, 1968) was the first book to be published about the rembetika songs and contributed in no small way to the myth of the rembetiko milieu. The virtue of the songs, for Petropoulos, was precisely their shady ambience and connections to the marginalized and the criminal demi-monde. The controversy about the rembetika, focused initially on the café aman music and later on the Piraeus style, is still alive today despite the general acceptance of the songs as the basis of much Greek popular music.

Within the circles of rembetika scholars and enthusiasts, issues of chronology, terminology and methodology are also debated. There are still serious gaps in our knowledge of the origins and early evolution of the genre despite considerable research into the historical background of the rembetika. We are not even sure if the word rembetiko is of Turkish origin as my early informers confidently asserted. On the subject of when the term was first used we are equally in the dark. The earliest instance of the term rembetiko as a designation for a particular type of song may have been on the labels of records pressed in the United States and England in the 1930s.[3] A recording made by Pol (Leopoldo Gad) in the USA, which almost certainly

[1] An account of the nationalism associated with the early rembetika and the Greek adaptation of Ottoman melodies and forms can be found in Risto Pennanen's article 'The Nationalization of Ottoman Popular Music in Greece', *Ethnomusicology*, 48/1, 2004, pp. 1–25.
[2] Ντ. Χριστιανόπουλος. «Ιστορική και αισθητική διαμόρφωση του ρεμπετικού τραγουδιού», *Διαγώνιος*, issue 1 (Jan. 1961), Thessaloniki, pp. 5–22.
[3] Stathis Gauntlett, *Carmina rebetika Graeciae recentioris*, Athens: Denise Harvey, 1985, pp. 31–2.

belongs to the late 1920s, is the earliest instance I know of, but a poster for the Neos Cosmos café for the year 1930 indicates that the Greek public were familiar with the term at that date. It advertises a programme of songs to be performed by Nouros and Stellakis which will include '...all the latest European and rembetika songs' as well as '*amanédhes*[1] full of pathos'.

The type of song later termed rembetiko may derive from or have its origins in an oral tradition where improvisation played an important part, but many of the early songs that are referred to or labelled rembetiko in Greek belonged to a late Ottoman tradition of café music. Older musicians I talked to confirm that they learnt their songs from amateur or semi-professional musicians who frequented the hashish dens and cafés of Piraeus. Some of the songs they called anonymous, others they ascribed to a particular musician, but they were not always in agreement about the authorship of such songs and they all remembered improvising not only music but also lyrics as they sat and played together. The improvised introductions to the songs, or '*taximia*', belong to a long tradition of Middle Eastern improvisation. It was in the *taximi* that a good musician showed his knowledge of the modal system and his dexterity, just as a singer displayed his or her musicianship in the vocal improvisations known as amanédhes (singular, *amané*) or *gazeler*.

When I wrote this book, it was difficult to hear the old café aman or Smyrna style rembetika. There were no long-playing records of the music available, and 78 r.p.m. records were hard to find in Athens. Since then there has been a proliferation of re-mastered early recordings. They have made us aware of the beauty and refinement of the music performed in the cafés aman and we can understand now what made the music so popular. If I had heard Rita Abatzi, for example, singing an amané, I might have written a different book. Ottoman café music, in Greece, western Turkey and the United States, was a rich, eclectic mixture, and its Greek performers, many of whom also recorded songs in Turkish, were splendid musicians. When the rembetika were first revived in the 1970s, the style of music then referred to as

---

[1] Italics will only be used the first time Greek words are introduced.

'Smyrna style' had long ceased to be popular. It was the bouzouki-based music of Piraeus, championed by Hadzidakis, Theodorakis, Petropoulos, and others, that seemed to be at the centre of the tradition. That the rembetika songs were prised from their exclusive environment and commercially exploited was to be expected of music performed in a rapidly-expanding city, especially after the first commercial recording companies were established in Greece. As Bruno Nettl said, 'What is it that sets urban musical cultures off from those of villages, small towns and nomadic life?... Perhaps most of all, it is the coming together of different musical styles and genres from many sources.'[1] In Greece it may only have been the poorest class of urban workers who were open to contact with the refugees from Smyrna and could freely borrow musical elements from whatever they heard around them. The earliest recordings of the rembetika bear witness to a healthy eclecticism you would expect of urban folk music. The commercial success of the rembetika meant that good musicians were encouraged to write songs in rembetika style. It also meant that as the lyrics lost their immediate contact with a lively sub-culture, composers began looking for new lyric-writers. The songs that the composers of the 1960s wrote using elements of the rembetika with the lyrics of Greece's leading poets may have been vastly different from the rembetika of the Piraeus underworld, but they were unthinkable without them.

What seemed to me like a faddish revival of the early rembetika in the 1970s has become a permanent recognition of the genre. Not only are there new clubs springing up in Athens where young people go to play and listen to the rembetika, but there are similar clubs in Sweden, Germany, the United States and Australia. The repertoire of these young musicians has changed too. At first they were determinedly purist and musicians rather solemnly imitated the nuances of vocal and instrumental style they had heard on records. Now the programmes often include a mixture of early rembetika and café aman style songs. Some clubs play traditional folk music as well. In fact the

---

[1] B. Nettl (ed.), *Eight Urban Musical Cultures: Tradition and Change.* Urbana: University of Illinois Press, 1978, p. 60.

mixture of music is not unlike what might have been heard in one of the early Athenian cafés aman.

The comparison I and other commentators have made between the rembetika and the blues of the USA seems to me to be validated by the lasting popularity of the rembetika and the freedom with which their forms have been adapted. The songs have strayed a long way from their musical and social origins. They have suffered a comparable period to the blues of rejection on moral and social grounds. They have been similarly modified to suit the tastes of a broader audience and later revived in a 'pure' style. Now that they are being performed in a variety of free and strict forms we begin to appreciate the best songs of early, middle, late or revival-style rembetika for what they are — good songs by any standards.

A number of the leading characters mentioned in this book have died since it was written, and I dedicate this new edition to their memory. Among them are the incomparable singer Sotiria Bellou, the most prolific of all rembetika composers Vassilis Tsitsanis, and the singer/songwriter Grigoris Bithikotsis, whom Theodorakis used to perform his popular songs during the 1960s. Sadly missed from the ranks of rembetika scholars is Ole Smith, whose recognition of the importance of the discography of the rembetika in the United States, amongst his other insights, made a lasting contribution to the field. Finally, my main informant, teacher and friend Thanassis Athanassiou has passed away. I hope he finds a little *mavraki* wherever he may be.

Gail Holst
Ithaca, 2006

Acknowledgements

A lot of people helped in the writing of this book, which was first published in 1975. Since then some of them have died. I would like, with this new edition, to remember with love and gratitude Thanassis Athanassiou, without whose help this book would never have been written, and Ted Petrides, who taught us all so much about the dances of Greece.

The Australia Council for the Arts was sufficiently enlightened to believe that research into Greek music was relevant to Australia.

Stathis Gauntlett, Peter Crowe, Willem Adriaansz, Yiorgos Samardzis and Vassilis Daramaras all helped me in Australia.

In Greece, so many people helped me that I can't thank them all, but I would like to thank some: Mikhailis Yenitsaris, Markos Dragoumis, Ilias Petropoulos, Vassilis Christianos, Ian Miller and Don Matthews all gave me useful information, and Kostas Hadzidoulis lent me valuable material from his archive; Alexandra allowed us to photograph instruments in her antique shop at 25 Adrianou Street in the old quarter of Athens; Maggie and Jack Sadoway helped me with preparing the manuscript, Louis Mohr read it with a careful eye, and finally I am deeply grateful to Denise Harvey for her thoughtful and creative editing.

*Map of Greece and Western Turkey showing
most of the towns and islands mentioned in the text.*

1

Turning on
to the rembetika

When I first came to Greece in 1966, I had hardly heard any Greek music and couldn't understand a word of Greek. I travelled about the countryside, especially in Crete, discovering village music and dancing, but I settled in the old Plaka quarter of Athens below the Acropolis, and it was the music of the city which I got to know best. I can't pretend to have landed on what I now regard as 'classic rembetika' with instinctive certainty. It was months before I began to sort out the various sounds of what the Greeks call *laïki* music, that is city popular music as opposed to country folk music.

The juke boxes of Athens were my real introduction to the rembetika. I had always felt a snobbish antipathy to juke boxes until I came to Greece, but then I began to regard them with real affection, and fed drachmas into them like a Las Vegas addict feeding nickels into a one-armed bandit. In 1966 you could find juke boxes all over Athens which were full of good rembetika records. Young men would come into a taverna, feed a handful of coins into the juke box and begin to dance, sometimes together, more often alone. This solo dance was unlike any dancing I'd ever seen — not exuberant, not being done for the joy of movement, not even sensual. It reminded me almost of a Quaker meeting, where only if the spirit moves does a man speak. The music would begin, the rhythm insistent, the voice harsh and metallic, and the dancer would rise as if compelled to make his statement. Eyes half-closed, in trance-like absorption, cigarette hanging from his lips, arms outstretched as if to keep his balance, he would begin to slowly circle. As the dance progressed, the movements would become more complex; there would be sudden feats of agility, swoops to the ground, leaps and twists, but the

Modern-style zebekiko in an Athens taverna.

dancer seemed to be feeling his way, searching for something, unsteady on his feet. The dance took place in public, people were watching it, and yet it appeared to be a private, introspective experience for the dancer. Sometimes there would be applause for the dancer, sometimes not, but the function of the dance was certainly not to entertain the company. It was as if the dance served as a sort of catharsis for the dancer, after which he sat down at his table and continued eating and drinking with renewed appetite.

I think it was through the dance that I came to the music of the rembetika, but it was very much a total experience. There was the sound of the bouzouki, which accorded so well with the slightly metallic voices of the singers, the words of the lyrics, which I slowly came to understand, and the half-western, half-eastern flavour of the melodies. Together they reminded me sometimes of flamenco, sometimes of the blues, sometimes of Turkish and Arabic music. And yet there were elements in this music which belonged to none of the others. The more I listened to the rembetika, the more I liked it, and the more I wanted to find out about it. This book is no more than a record of some of the discoveries I made on my way.

On my journey into the rembetika I met some *rembetes*,[1] read what little had been written about it in Greek, listened to a lot of music and studied the bouzouki and the *baglama*, the principal

[1] The word *rembetis* (plural *rembetes*) is used to refer to a man who lived the life of the sub-culture in which rembetika music was played. It is a little more specific than the word *mangas* (see note on page 21).

18

instruments of the rembetika. What I learned was perhaps enough to say what I'm sure the rembetika are not. What I think they are may come indirectly out of the characters, conversations and songs I've selected. I'd like to be able to avoid definitions: they tend to be meaningless and to lead people away from rather than towards the music. For those who like them however, here are a few made by rembetika scholars. They say something about the rembetika: not enough and too much.

'The rembetika are small simple songs sung by simple people.' Ilias Petropoulos.[1]

'Songs of the Greek urban sub-proletariat from the end of the 19th century to the 1950s...'. Olivier Revault d'Allonnes.[2]

'An expression of the artistic potential of the masses of the subproletariat of Greek towns.' Stathis Damianakos.[3]

'The rembetis...is the suffering, wronged, hunted man — the rembetika were written for him.' Tassos Skhorelis and Mikis Ekonomides.[4]

The only definition of the rembetika that I like, not because it tells you any more but because it has a little charm, is that of the old rembetika composer, Rovertakis himself, as recorded in Skhorelis and Ekonomides's biography: 'Rembetika songs were written by rembetes for rembetes... The rembetis was a man who had a sorrow and threw it out.'

In 1966, 1 found it hard to talk to many Greeks about the rembetika. The middle-class, educated Greeks I met told me they weren't interested in that sort of music — it was old, Turkish style music — didn't I like the new music of Theodorakis and Hadzidakis? Yes, I said, I was enthusiastic about it, particularly the music

---

[1] *Ρεμπέτικα Τραγούδια*, Athens, 1968, p. 11.
[2] 'L'art contre la société. Une culture dominée: Le rébétiko', in *La création artistique et les promesses de la liberté*. Paris: Klincksieck, 1973, p. 144.
[3] *Κοινωνιολογία του ρεμπέτικου*. Athens: Ermeias, 1976, p. 141.
[4] *Ένας ρεμπέτης — Γιώργος Ροβερτάκης «Σαμιωτάκι»*. Athens: Rembetiko Arheio 2, 1973.

19

of Theodorakis, but this rembetika music was something else. I wanted to know more about it. Where could I hear more of it? Oh, you go *sta bouzoukia — that* is where you hear the rembetika.

Every time I went 'to the bouzoukis' I regretted it and I became convinced that it was impossible to hear the rembetika in a modern bouzouki club. If you were looking for a kitsch night out and had plenty of cash with you, you may get some enjoyment from a night at

*Turning on to rembetika. The author playing baglama
while the 'Teacher' plays bouzouki.*

the bouzoukis. You could pop balloons, smash plates brought in special piles to the table for the purpose and costing much more than they were worth, drink any imported liquor you liked (if you could afford it) but not find a drop of good barrelled *retsina*, watch young drunken boys and their girl friends pay to dance badly, or groups of professional dancers perform balletic travesties of rembetika dances, and have your ear drums permanently damaged by over-amplified bouzoukis. Worse still, you could watch a great rembetika singer like Sotiria Bellou sitting tiredly in the midst of the circus, beefing out the songs which had made her famous.

Greeks who thought they were in the know about the rembetika, especially those who considered themselves to be *manges*,[1] were not much more helpful than the bourgeois Greeks. Some were, I'm sure, quite genuine in their enthusiasm for the rembetika. One was a fine *zebekiko* dancer, another had made a lengthy study of the rembetika, all of them collected old rembetika records. But when I asked them what the rembetika were, or what the characteristics of a mangas were, they came up with a bewildering mass of conflicting information. This is a small sample:

'The rembetes are all dead now.'

'I'm a rembetis.'

'Rembetes and manges are the same...but different.'

'You have to be a hashish smoker to be a rembetis.'

'The real rembetes were all in the underworld.'

'The true rembetes are all nice fellows who love their friends, never touch hashish and hardly ever get drunk.'

'The true rembetis has to be bi-sexual.'

'Real rembetes were good family men.'

'Rembetes don't marry but have mistresses.'

'Rembetes all carried knives, and if they once pulled one out they didn't put it away until they'd used it.'

'The rembetes were gentle, peace-loving people.'

'Mangas means you've got a lot of money and you throw it around.'

'The rembetes were all poor.'

'The rembetika began in 1922.'

'There were always the rembetika in Greece.'

---

[1] The *manges* (singular *mangas* — the pronunciation of the 'g' is hard in both plural and singular) were men who formed a sub-culture on the fringe of society. Many of them were actually in the underworld. The nearest equivalents in English in the same period were probably 'spivs', 'wide-boys' or 'hep-cats'.

When I left Greece in 1968, I had a confused idea of what the rembetika were, a handful of rembetika records, and a copy of the first and only sizeable book to be published in Greece on the rembetika — Ilias Petropoulos's *Rembetika Tragoudhia*. It was in Australia, homesick for Greece and like so many people who loved the country, feeling that it was impossible to go back there until the political situation changed,[1] that I began looking more deeply into the rembetika. My Greek was improving and I read my way through Petropoulos's book, which was a lively, if limited introduction to the rem-

Sotiria Bellou in 1950.

betika, containing the lyrics of over two hundred rembetika songs. I wore out the records I had of Sotiria Bellou; for me she is still the best of the female rembetika singers, with a voice as deep as a man's and as full of pain as Billie Holiday's. Bellou lived hard, served time in jail, earned a lot of money, and spent a lot of it helping other musicians. She may have been performing in noisy, garish night-clubs, but her voice remained as good as ever. Her version of 'San pethano sto karavi' — 'If I die on the boat' — makes my hair stand on end, although I must have listened to it a thousand times.

Towards the end of the dictatorship there was a revival of interest in early rembetika music in Greece. In 1949, Manos Hadzidakis had presented the rembetika to the bourgeoisie of Athens in his famous lecture at the Arts Theatre of Athens, telling his startled audience that Vassilis Tsitsanis, the famous rembetika musician, was the Bach of Greece. Markos Vamvakaris and Sotiria Bellou performed rembetika

[1] Following a coup d'état in 1967, Greece was ruled by a military dictatorship until 1974.

songs at the lecture, which sparked a heated exchange of articles in the Greek press. Some critics were shocked. Others acknowledged the power and charm of the rembetika songs. In 1960, Mikis Theodorakis had presented a cycle of songs based on Yiannis Ritsos's poem, 'Epitafios'. They were not only composed in rembetika style, but more daring than Hadzidakis, Theodorakis used the rembetika song-writer and singer Grigoris Bithikotsis to interpret the songs, accompanied by the bouzouki-player Manolis Hiotis. Even Hadzidakis, who had championed the rembetika, did not dream of combining it with high-brow poetry. The question of the true value of the rembetika, and in particular their 'Greekness', was hotly debated in the press, but the success of Theodorakis's rembetika-based songs was such that it was difficult to argue that they were irrelevant.

The military dictatorship of 1967–74 banned all of Theodorakis's music as well as the poetry of Ritsos. Theodorakis spent the dictatorship in prison, under house arrest and later in exile, and Ritsos remained under house arrest throughout the period. By the early 1970s, it was difficult for young Greeks to hear the old-style rembetika. The 78 r.p.m. recordings of performers like Markos Vamvakaris had mostly disappeared, and the modern 'rembetika' recordings were debased versions of the rembetika which they rightly rejected. Ilias Petropoulos's book about the rembetika was published in 1968 and immediately banned, making it a collector's item that began to circulate underground. It was entertainingly written and dealt with the whole social milieu of the rembetes. The words of songs which had been banned for years reminded young Greeks that the rembetes were drop-outs, anti-authoritarian, and even better, they smoked marihuana. Suddenly the rembetika seemed with-it, daring music. Where could you hear these songs, meet these characters Petropoulos described? The craze had come just a few years too late for most of them. Three of the greatest rembetika figures died within a year of each other — Stratos Payioumdzis, Yiannis Papaioannou, and Markos Vamvakaris, who fortunately dictated his autobiography to Angeliki Kail shortly before he died.[1] Petropoulos and a number of rembetika

[1] Vamvakaris, Markos, with Angeliki Vellou-Kail. *Αυτοβιογραφία*. Athens: Papazisis, 1978.

23

enthusiasts persuaded some of the older rembetika musicians, including Rosa Eskenazi, Kostas Roukounas and Prodromos Tsaousakis, to perform in small venues in the Plaka without undue amplification. The response was so enthusiastic that two of them, Mikhailis Yenitsaris and Yiorgos Mouflouzelis, made a comeback and others followed in their footsteps, filling small night-clubs for years with the sounds of the old rembetika.

Perhaps there was something in the swaggering individuality and the pain expressed in the rembetika, the contemptuous references to the police and the secret language of the hashish smokers, which appealed to a population living in a military-police state. Perhaps the rembetika spoke to the young people of the 70s in a way they understood. Whatever the reasons for the resurgence of interest in the early rembetika, the result was that a number of old recordings which had been unavailable or hard to get were copied or remade on long-playing records. At last the voices of the 20s and 30s could be heard and the rembetika I was looking for became easy to find.

In Australia I had access to some old 78 r.p.m. recordings but they were in such bad condition that the sound was more tantalizing than enjoyable. Then I discovered Yiorgos Samardzis, an old bouzouki player from the island of Mytilini who had played with Markos in his youth and who remembered a lot of songs from the pre-war period. Nobody had asked him to play them for years, although he had been playing in Greek clubs in Australia ever since he'd left Greece twenty years before. We sat for days in my house in Sydney while he played and the songs rose slowly out of his memory...

'When I was a little boy,' he said, 'my father wouldn't let me listen to bouzouki music, but I heard that Markos was coming to play in Mytilini[1] and I was determined to go and hear him...so two of us from the village, we walked all the way on our bare feet — it was twenty kilometres, and we were all dusty when we got there and we had no money to get in. We hung around outside...they finally let us stand on the edge and we heard it all. We got into terrible trouble when we got home, but I knew I had to play the bouzouki. And then

---

[1] Mytilini is the common name for the island of Lesbos as well as its capital city.

I got very sick…I was in bed for years, and they let me have a bouzouki — by then we had some records of rembetika songs, and I lay
in bed and imitated them…'.

And Yiorgos went on playing with nothing but his bouzouki, beating time with his foot, singing in a voice that was rough and sweet,
and I felt that the journey into the rembetika had really begun — we
were in a small dark *teké* or hashish den in Piraeus, with the *narghilé*
being passed around from one rembetis to another, and the sweet
black hashish fumes filling the air. A rembetis with a sorrow was
throwing it out in song.

Crazy Nick and Marinos the Moustache enjoying a coffee and a nargilé.

2

Piraeus in the 1920s — the road starts

If you get off a boat at Piraeus and walk towards the railway station, you pass a large slab of concrete with a statue of Karaiskakis, one of the heroes of the 1821 Greek War of Independence, in the middle of it. You can't miss him because he has a fine moustache and is sitting on a rearing horse. If you had got off a boat in Piraeus in say 1929 and walked by the same route, you would have found, in place of the square with the statue, a huddle of small houses and shops. In one of the small shops you could have drunk a thick, sweet cup of Turkish coffee and ordered a water pipe or narghilé, which the proprietor would lift carefully off a shelf and light with a few coals from the charcoal brazier. Men with fine moustaches would be sitting on rush-bottomed chairs, playing with their amber worry-beads and talking of the difficulty of finding a job, or of their lost houses and lands in Turkey.

From one of the nearby shops you might hear the faint sound of music, and if you asked Crazy Nick or Marinos the Moustache, they might take you to hear Yiorgos Batis playing the tiny baglama to his friends in a teké. There the manges would be sitting on the floor around a charcoal brazier while a boy filled the narghilé with Turkish hashish and passed it around. Batis might begin to play an improvised taximi in the mode of rast,[1] and then break into a song of his own or one of Papazoglou the Cucumber's. Unless you were a mangas yourself, you would find it difficult to understand all the words because they would be largely slang — rather like the jive you might have heard on a Harlem pavement at the same time:

[1] *Rast* is the name of one of the modes used in rembetika music. The modes are discussed on pp. 77–9.

27

...Down in Lemonadhika they caught a couple of cabbage-sellers, (i.e. pickpockets). *They put the irons* (handcuffs*) on them and they're taking them to the narrow* (jail) *and if they don't find the cabbage* (wallet) *they'll eat wood* (get a beating)....

During the song, one of the manges, already very high, might get up slowly to dance. As he circles and sways, the others smoke and sing, and Batis plucks sad sweet notes from his little instrument, while the harsh life of Piraeus in the 20s is forgotten in a rembetika dream.

Although a small number of recordings of rembetika-style music were made outside Greece, in America and Turkey, as early as the first decade of the century, Piraeus in the 1920s was the cradle of a new rembetika style dominated by the bouzouki. The real beginnings of the rembetika certainly go back well into the 19th century, but since they belong to an oral tradition, we can only make guesses about what the music was like. One guess we can make is that the rembetika appeared towards the end of the 19th century in a number of urban centres where Greeks lived. About this time musical cafés appeared in towns like Athens and Piraeus, Larissa, Hermoupolis, on the island of Syros, Thessaloniki, which remained under Turkish domination until 1912, Smryna, on the Turkish coast, and Constantinople. These cafés were of various types, but one was called the café aman, probably a corruption of the Turkish *mani kahvesi*, a café where two or three singers improvised on verses, often in the form of a dialogue with free rhythm and melody. In Turkish the form was called *gazel*, and the verses on which the singer improvised were taken from the repertoire of Ottoman 'Divan' poetry. Many of the early rembetika singers also recorded such vocal improvisations or amanédhes, which displayed the singer's skill and knowledge of Ottoman modal music. Greek musicians performing these amanédhes generally used sad verses in Greek that looked back with nostalgia to the lost world of Greek Asia Minor. Kostas Roukounas, a composer and singer who performed in various styles — demotic, café aman and rembetika — recorded a large number of amanédhes, as did Stratos Payioumdzis, Rosa Eskenazi and Rita Abatzi.

In the early Greek cafés aman, there would simply be a space left at one end of the café for musicians. Wandering street players, many of them gypsies, would play in the café for a short time and then move on. Later, small orchestras called *koumpanies* became permanently attached to a café. They were made up of partly Turkish and partly Greek traditional instruments like the *santouri*, a hammered dulcimer with over a hundred strings played with little wooden wands, the *kanonaki*, a type of plucked zither, the violin, the *laouto*, or folk lute, and the *outi* (the classical Arab *'ud*). Women would frequently perform in the cafés aman as singers and dancers. They would use finger cymbals and tambourines to emphasize the rhythm of the dance. The commonest dance performed was the *tsifteteli*, the dance later known as the belly dance. Other dances included the *kasaska*, a sort of imitation Cossack dance; the *allegro*, also Slavic in style; and the zebekiko, which became the principal dance of the rembetika.

The music which was being played in the cafés aman was important for the development of the rembetika, but there was another style

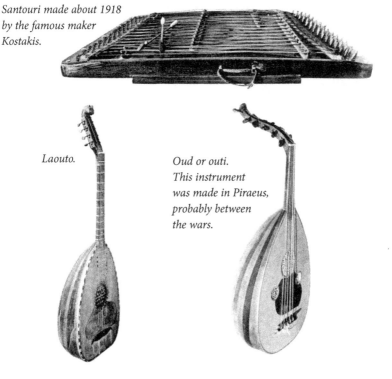

Santouri made about 1918 by the famous maker Kostakis.

Laouto.

Oud or outi. This instrument was made in Piraeus, probably between the wars.

29

Nikos Mathesis (Crazy Nick), a well-known Piraeus underworld character. Mathesis wrote several rembetika songs and was reputed to have killed at least one man.

Photograph taken in Piraeus, 1928.

of music emerging simultaneously with the café aman music which was to be influential in the formation of the mature rembetika style. Ever since the Greek War of Independence, the political situation in Greece had been unstable, to say the least. The sad memoirs of General Makriyannis, who had been a hero during the war and who died in poverty, having been imprisoned and humiliated, give a picture of the corruption, repression and violence which marked Greek political life until the last quarter of the 20th century.[1] From the time of the first king of modern Greece, Otto of Bavaria (1832–62), the Greek prisons were full of political as well as common criminals. In the prisons, instruments were made and songs were composed. The easiest instru-

[1] General Makriyannis's memoirs have been translated into English (*Makriyannis*, edited and translated by H. A. Liddderdale, Oxford, 1966).

ment to make and to hide, because of its small size, was the baglama. A gourd could be substituted for a wooden sound box, and then all you needed was a length of wood for a handle, pieces of gut to use as frets and wire for the strings.

The jail songs continued to be sung outside the prisons, and although at one time both they and the instruments associated with them — baglama and bouzouki — were banned, the music became popular in the underworld circles of the Greek towns. The underworld, during the period from the end of the 19th century to the Second World War, was a much less clearly defined phenomenon than we think of it today. In a corrupt, repressive society, where the police were easily bribed, and electoral candidates all employed agents to buy voters, to be against the law was often simply a natural concomitant of urban poverty. A large number of terms were used to refer to the loosely united groups of men who were on the fringes of society — the *koutsavakidhes*, the manges, the *vlamidhes*, the *tsiftes*, the rembetes.[1] References to these groups are found in writers of the period such as the short-story writer and novelist from the island of Skiathos, Alexandros Papadiamandis, and the prose writer and poet Andreas Karkavitsas, as well as in the rembetika songs. Persecution of these characters, especially of the koutsavakidhes, who seem to have been particularly colourful with provocatively eccentric costumes — it was fashionable to wear one's jacket with only the left arm through the sleeve and the other arm left free in case of a knife fight — became especially strong under the legendary Baraktaris, a hated Athenian police chief. The now fashionable Kolonaki Square was once a favourite haunt of these young studs, who swaggered and strutted, talking their private slang.

One of the common features of the marginal society and the jail society was the smoking of hashish. In Turkish towns, hashish was both legal and commonly used. In Greece, laws against the smoking and sale of hashish were promulgated in 1890, but not strictly

---

[1] The terms are loosely used, but *koutsavakidhes* were tough men who seem to have engaged in frequent knife-fights. *Vlamidhes* were also toughs, and the word *tsiftis* (plural *tsiftes*), originally meant mate or friend. All these words were later subsumed into the terms mangas or rembetis.

enforced for at least another thirty years. The small establishments where hashish was smoked, usually through a narghilé, or hubble-bubble, were called *tekédhes* (the plural form of teké). In the areas of Troumba in Piraeus and Barra in Thessaloniki, there were well-known tekédhes, a number of which are mentioned by name in rembetika songs. Sidheris's teké in Thessaloniki is mentioned, for example, in the song 'I Dhrosoula' — 'The Dew'. The music performed in these tekédhes was, by the turn of the century, already

Police chief Baraktaris.

a form of the rembetika. *Baglamadhes* and bouzoukis were becoming standard instruments and the themes of the songs were those of jail, the underworld and hashish.

At this time, two new characters appeared in the shadow puppet theatre of Greece, the *Karaghiozis*, a form of popular entertainment which has always reflected important social and political currents in Greek life. Stavrakas, the mangas, and Nondas, the young urban worker, first made their appearance in the Karaghiozis repertoire in about 1905. But although the world of the manges, described in many of the rembetika songs, seems to have been established by the first decade of the 20th century, it was an unexpected outside event that caused it to flourish and to centre itself in Piraeus.

Modern Greek history is dominated by the theme of the '*Megali Idhea*' — the Great Idea — that is, the recapture of the jewel of Byzantine civilization and the spiritual centre of the Greek Orthodox Church, Constantinople. Ever since its surrender to the Turks in 1453, the Greeks have dreamed of 'The City', as it is still referred to by Greeks today, returning to Greek hands. The Smyrna disaster, or as it is sometimes called, the 'Massacre of Smyrna', was a direct consequence of this grandiose, impossible dream. The events of the Turko-Greek war which ended in 1922 are well known. The Greek government had made what it considered a firm agreement with its allies, particularly with Britain's Prime Minister Lloyd George, to support the Greek army in an attempt to invade the hinterland of Smyrna, using that Greek port as a base. The troops marched almost unopposed towards Ankara, but the allies failed to support them, and they had entirely underestimated the strength of the young Kemal Ataturk's forces. When they eventually did engage the Turkish troops, the Greeks were defeated and forced to withdraw over hostile territory with no adequate supply lines. As they retreated, frightened Orthodox inhabitants of the area, fearing Turkish reprisals, abandoned their farms and joined the soldiers converging on the already overcrowded port of Smyrna. In the confusion which followed, the town was set on fire, and thousands died in the flames or leapt into the sea where allied ships, for fear of offending the Turks, refused to come to their aid.

The outcome of this futile war between Turkey and Greece was a compulsory exchange of populations between the two countries. The criterion for nationality was religion: if you were Orthodox you were declared Greek; if you were Muslim you were declared Turkish. The 'Greek' refugees numbered over a million. Many of them had lived for generations in Turkey, spoke Turkish as their first and sometimes only language, and had no desire to be uprooted. Even before the Smyrna incident, there had been a wave of nervous immigratio — now there was a flood of homeless, jobless refugees who swelled the total population of Greece by at least twenty-five per cent. In a small, under-developed country like Greece, this sudden influx could not possibly be absorbed without hardship. Attempts were made to settle some of the refugees on the land, but the bulk of them crowded into the cities, particularly Athens and Piraeus, where although industrial development was well behind the rest of Europe, some possibilities for employment existed.

The refugees brought with them the skills and refinements of a more sophisticated society, but it was some years before most of them could make use of their talents. As the rembetika musician Yiorgos Rovertakis remembered (he was twelve years old when the incident happened, his father having been a horse-dealer in Smyrna), 'We lived for six months in someone's yard — like dogs. Then we were put into huts built by the State.'

In the years following the exchange of populations, a series of shanty settlements grew up in a belt around Athens, settlements with nostalgic names like New Ionia and New Smyrna. The refugees brought a style of music with them which was already enjoying some popularity in the cafés aman. Because so many of the Greek refugees were from the city of Smyrna the music they brought to the mainland is often referred to as 'Smyrna-style' music. New cafés sprang up where musicians from Istanbul, Aivali, on the west coast of Turkey, and Smyrna, played and sang. One of the most famous of these cafés was the Mikrasia on Piraeos Street, one of the main streets of Athens leading from Omonia Square, which was to become the headquarters of the first association of popular musicians in Greece — the Association of Athenian and Piraeus Musicians, formed under the initiative of one of the Smyrna refugees, Emmanuel Chrissafakis.

The refugees may not have been part of the underworld, but they were living on the edge of Greek society, competing for jobs in poor urban areas, segregated often by language as well as customs from the bulk of the Greek population who resented their presence. It was not surprising that many of them joined the rembetes or manges in their loosely-organized sub-culture, or were attracted to the hashish-smoking tekédhes, to which they were accustomed in Turkey. Nor was it surprising that the rembetika musicians in Greece should have been attracted by the technical skills and professionalism of the Smyrna musicians. Names of such Asia Minor refugees as Yiannis Dragatsis, Dimitrios Semsis, Panayiotis Toundas, Kostas Skarvelis, Stellakis Perpiniadis and Andonis Dalgas soon became synonymous with the musical life of Athens and all included songs of low life in their repertoire, songs which came to be termed 'Asia Minor rembetika' or 'Smyrneïka'. Women singers who became famous in the café aman scene included Marika Politissa, Rita Abatzi and Rosa Eskenazi.

Of the various styles of music performed in the cafés, some songs may have originated in anonymous jail and hashish-smoking songs of the underworld, but many new songs were composed to cater to what was obviously a growing taste for such lyrics. A number of refugee musicians chose to adopt the world of the manges and began performing with rembetika musicians in Piraeus. Just how important the influx of refugees was to the development of the rembetika is hard to say, but ten years after their arrival, the rembetika had moved out of the narrow world of the tekédhes and was becoming popular city music. Songs which had been handed down by an oral tradition were now being written down and recorded, while new songs were being composed in the rembetika style.

We are now back to where we began this chapter, in Piraeus in 1930. This is a convenient, arbitrary date for setting the beginning of what might be called 'classical' or 'Piraeus-style' rembetika. It coincides roughly with the earliest commercial recordings made in Greece by H.M.V., Columbia and Odeon. Men like Yiannis Papaioannou, Stratos Payioumdzis, Stellakis Perpiniadis, Markos Vamvakaris, Anestis Delias and Yiorgos Batis were all about to become the leaders of the new style of rembetika, which already had a history but was only beginning to have a wide public.

A Smyrna-style trio: Rosa Eskenazi with the violinist Semsis and Tomboulis.

A group of rembetes and refugees in the fish-market at Piraeus in 1937. The instrumentalist on the left is the brilliant saz-player, Iovan Tsaous, and on his left is Mathesis.

3

The world of a rembetis — Markos Vamvakaris

By setting the 'classical' period of the rembetika in a teké in Piraeus, I will already have offended a number of rembetika musicians and admirers. There were musicians, good rembetika musicians like Rovertakis and Roukounas, who never smoked hashish or knew what the inside of a teké looked like, but they were not rembetes or manges in the usual sense of the words. Most of the manges smoked, especially the musicians; most of the early rembetika songs deal directly or indirectly with hashish, and a good part of the *mangika*, or mangas slang, is secret hashish language. Once hashish-smoking was prosecuted by the police, the manges became a closer-knit society. They already shared common tastes, occupations, habits — now they had a bond of common abuse, and a musical tradition to express it in. Pre-war rembetika centred in Piraeus is largely hashish music. It is more than that, but it flows outward from the tekédhes of Piraeus into the surrounding society. So without further apology I will take you back into that Piraeus teké — to Mikhailis's teké in Hiotika, where the best manges went — and we'll meet some of the manges and listen to their music.

From the outside, all you see is a small wooden cottage, a few huts tacked together. In the back rooms, the family live. The front room is larger, and almost bare of furniture. There is a dirt floor with a few low seats. Mikhailis has a fire going — he's burning thyme. Thyme is the sweetest wood with which to light the narghilé, but almond will do, or walnut. There's a charcoal brazier in the centre of the room, and the atmosphere is heavy with smoke. Four men are already smoking a narghilé. Not the elegant glass narghilé of the cafés, but a crude pipe made out of a coconut. The proprietor, or *tekedzis*, brings another narghilé and sits down to warm a piece of hashish over the charcoal brazier.

'Hey, Mikhaili,[1] have you heard about the stuff Uncle Yiannis brought in from Itea? It'll send you off your head with two puffs they told me.'

Mikhailis looks unimpressed: 'The best hashish is from Bursa, the Turkish stuff. You pay more for it, but it's worth it. I've been smoking since I was a kid. Egyptian, Bulgarian, the lot, and this is the best stuff you'll ever get.'

He takes the little packet wrapped in grease-proof paper away from the fire and begins crushing it on the floor. When it's soft and cool, he breaks off a piece of the dark brown hashish and places it carefully in the bowl of the narghilé.

There is a faint noise outside and Mikhailis looks up anxiously, but his wife has been watching and calls out: 'It's only Batis and Markos.'

Two men walk in, the first a small, natty man with a neat moustache and a baglama under one arm.

'I've brought my little gypsy friend in for a smoke,' he says, waving the tiny instrument. 'And who have we here? It's Crazy Nick and Yiannis the Cabby — and Marinos the Moustache. How are your whiskers tonight? Aren't you boys going to give your old friend Batis a smoke?'

The manges grin, and hand a pipe to the little man. He sits down next to Crazy Nick and calls out to his friend, 'Hey, Marko, what are you doing standing around? Sit down and have a drag.'

The big man, who's wearing a smart suit with a working man's cap, sits down beside him, putting his bouzouki carefully behind him. He takes the pipe and pulls deeply; so far he hasn't spoken, and his heavy, jowly face has remained as expressionless as a St Bernard's. A few more puffs and his eyes begin to hood. There's a hint of a smile around his mouth. He reaches for the bouzouki and strikes a few notes... 'Bravo Marko-boy with your lovely bouzouki,' mutters Crazy Nick, and Markos wanders through the introduction, improvising and ornamenting as he goes. Wild rushes of notes, then slow, climbing passages, then back to the note he started on, and again and again

[1] Mikhailis/Mikhaili, Markos/Marko: masculine names ending in 's' in Greek drop the 's' in the vocative and accusative cases.

he hits that note as if he can't get away from it, and breaks off, but only to catch it again, this time beating out a rhythm with his foot on the floor. After the complex introduction, the song is surprisingly simple. Batis joins in with his baglama, while Markos, in a gravely voice, sings the song he made up last night...

> *Make it, Stavro, make it. Set it alight and burn it.*
> *Give it to Crazy Nick, the high of the carpenter.*
> *Take a drag, Yanni, the manges' teké-man.*
> *Give it to our little Nick to take away his troubles.*
> *Give our Batis a turn, our street boy, our rascal.*

Markos Vamvakaris photographed in 1967, shortly before his death. He is holding his cigarette in traditional bouzouki-player fashion.

'Bravo Marko with your bouzouki! Mikhaili, wash out the pipe and make a fresh narghilé for our mangas, Marko!'

The manges in Mikhailis's teké that night in 1930 knew that they were with a man who played good music and made up good songs about them. They probably never suspected that Markos Vamvakaris would become known as the father of the rembetika. Nor did they dream that the music of the secret hashish dens of Piraeus would become so popular that all classes of Greek society would flock to hear it, or that bouzouki players would one day drive Rolls-Royces.

Markos Vamvakaris was born in 1905 in a poor village on the island of Syros. Syros is one of the few areas of Greece where there is a sizable Catholic population. The Catholics from Syros are known as Frankosyriani, a word which was to become familiar to most Greeks through Markos's famous song, 'The Frankosyrian Girl'. Markos's father played the *gaida*, or Greek bagpipes, and his grandfather used-to like to write songs. The whole island was full of music — there were santouri players, violinists, drummers, and even bouzouki players, but the music was *dhimotiki*, or folk music, and it was played mostly

 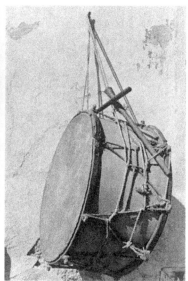

Gaida.   *Greek drum.*

at one time of the year, at the carnival of Apokreas, the two weeks preceding Orthodox Lent. Then the young men would dance the special zebekiko of Syros, with their knives and their bright costumes, while the *laterna*, or barrel-organ, covered in decorations, would tinkle out music that excited Markos so much he would go and press his ear to the instrument, often getting a sharp kick from the organ grinder. Or his father would play his bagpipes in the cafés, and Markos would accompany him on the small ceramic hand-drum or *darbouka*, collecting the few drachmas which the family so badly needed.

When he was only eight years old, Markos had to leave school and work with his mother in a cotton thread factory while his father served in the army. He hated being in the factory and the girls teased him for his big feet. He was bored with making little paper packets, so he ran away and wandered about the streets. After working in a grocer's shop and a butcher's shop, he got a job in a newspaper office, selling papers, and it was here that he began mixing with the local underworld characters — gamblers, pimps, petty thieves. It was here, too, that he first became acquainted with hashish, for some of the best

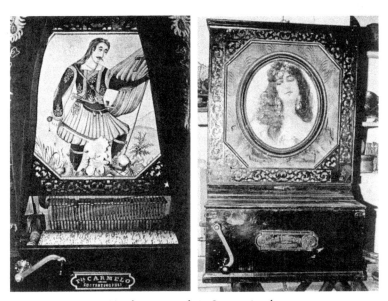

Two laternas made in Constantinople.

Greek hashish was grown on Syros. As the black market grew up during the war, Markos did well. His father and his uncle were dealing in tobacco and sugar, and Markos was charging high prices for newspapers, which were scarce and eagerly snatched up by the local population, but it wasn't long before the police caught up with them, and the whole family went to prison.

At fifteen, Markos stowed away on a ship for Piraeus, and got a job loading coal on the wharves. In those days, Piraeus was a tough, open port, full of bums, criminals, gamblers, whores and hashish. Markos

Markos (left) with his sister and the brother he later quarrelled violently with.

was soon living the life of many of the dock-workers: hard, dirty work all day, women and hashish at night. He was kept in smart clothes by an older whore, and did the rounds of the tekédhes each night.

His family followed him to Piraeus, and seeing the life he was leading, his two younger brothers began mixing with the underworld too. One brother took up smoking and began to have hallucinations. He soon became mad and died on the streets. The other brother became a knife-carrying tough, eventually killed a man in a fight, and spent the rest of his life in jail. Markos himself was jailed several times, the first time only for a few days after he had been caught in a teké. And no sooner did he get out of jail than he was back in the tekédhes. Life for the manges was hard, and the narghilé was sweet. If you smoked a pipe with your friends, you forgot for a while the tough world outside. Markos was also trying to forget his new wife who nagged him and went with other men, and the depressing sight of the refugees swarming Piraeus with their bundles of belongings and their hungry children. The alternative to the narghilé was alcohol, and that made you angry, ready for a fight. The manges who smoked rarely fought. They went to the teké for peace, sometimes to listen to a little music. Then they would eat and dance and drink a little in the cafés. As it became more and more dangerous to smoke in the tekédhes, they would go to the caves on the waterfront at Piraeus, or up to the mountains where there would be a narghilé hidden in a cave or in the branches of some tree. There they could smoke without fear.

It was while Markos was working in a slaughter-house, about 1925, that he first heard Old Nikos from Aivali play the bouzouki. From that night on he was as hooked on the bouzouki as he was on hashish. 'I'll cut my hands off if I don't get a bouzouki,' he told his father. It wasn't the first time he had heard the bouzouki — there were bouzouki players in Syros — but Old Nikos played in a style that was new to him. He had spent ten years in jail, and played heavy Turkish-style zebekika with improvised introductions, or taximia. The music spoke to Markos from the world of prison and hashish and he began to imitate the style as soon as he found a bouzouki. Six months after his first meeting with Old Nikos, he had learnt enough to play the music in the tekédhes and delight the manges as they smoked. Nikos, passing by a teké and hearing the sound of a bouzouki, stood listening for a while, wondering who could be playing such music. When he saw the boy he'd met six months earlier, he knew there was nothing he could teach him. He was already a musician.

In those days, Markos was not the only musician playing in the tekédhes. He soon met 'Boyadzis', Yiannis the Glasses, 'Alekaki' and 'Memetis', and Iovan Tsaous who played a *saz* in a manner which no one else could play. At Gravaras's luxurious teké in Menidhi, he listened to a pianist called Manolis the Turk, who played rembetika music regularly, while the manges smoked and ate sweet cakes.

The refugees who arrived in 1922 had brought with them a style of music which was new to many Greeks, and a style of entertainment that would change the pattern of Athenian social life. In Smyrna and Constantinople, Greeks were accustomed to going out at night with their families and listening to music. In Athens and Piraeus, men usually went out alone except in the most sophisticated circles. In the late 20s and 30s, cafés of various types, like the café aman and the café chantant,[1] sprang up around Athens and Piraeus. The music which was played in them was mostly Smyrna-style music — tsifteteli, *aivaliotiko*, *syrtos*, amané. Musicians like Kostas Karipis, Andonios Diamantides ('Dalgas') and Agapios Tomboulis became popular, but generally the music of the cafés remained apart from the world of the rembetika. The two styles occasionally overlapped, and the rembetika musicians could not help but be influenced by the superior technical skill and theoretical knowledge of the Smyrna musicians. A number of refugees chose to join the rembetika circles, and either took up bouzouki or brought their own instruments with them into the tekédhes.

One of the most interesting of the refugee musicians was a young boy called Anestis Delias, known as Artemis. He was only eight years old when his parents fled from Smyrna and settled in the Drapetsona quarter of Piraeus. His father was a well-known musician in Smyrna who played the santouri and was called the 'Black Cat'. From his father Artemis learned the guitar, and by the time he was sixteen he was already an accomplished player. He was also frequenting the local tekédhes and mixing with the rembetes. It was in a teké that he met Markos and Batis, who had already teamed up with the third member of what was to become a famous quartet. Stratos Payioumdzis, known as Stratos the Lazy, was also from Asia Minor, although his family had emigrated to Greece some time before the disaster. He was the singer of the quartet, a soft-faced fellow who

---

[1] In broad terms, the cafés chantant tended towards a more European repertoire, whereas the cafés aman were where patrons went to hear the more 'oriental' or Smyrna-style music. It is not clear, however, how strict the distinction was.

The great quartet of early rembetika musicians: from left to right, Stratos, Markos, Batis and Artemis.

talked too much and was always being teased by the manges for his chatter and his singing. In those days he would sing Markos's songs, while Markos played and Batis strummed a few notes on his baglama. Batis was the clown of the group. A Piraeus-born second-hand dealer, older than the others and with a few drachmas in his pocket to lend them when they were broke, he loved music and old instruments. He owned a number of bouzoukis and baglamas, all of which he gave pet names to, and when he died in 1967 his favourite baglama was buried with him. Batis doesn't seem to have been much of a player, but he was always welcome in manges circles because of his quick tongue and his generosity.

By the mid-30s the four musicians, Markos, Stratos, Batis and Artemis, were playing together almost every night in the tekédhes, and they were soon asked to play in a small courtyard belonging to a man called Constantopoulos. Artemis and Markos were both beginning to make records, and people came from all over Athens to listen to them play in the club. Batis's song 'Secretly in a boat I went', first

45

recorded in 1935 by Stratos, describes the friends smoking together in the cave of Drakos (Dragon), off the Piraeus coast:

> *Secretly in a boat I went*
> *and came out at Dragon's cave.*
> *I saw three men stoned on hashish*
> *stretched out on the sand.*
>
> *It was Batis and Artemis*
> *and Stratos the lazy one.*
> *Hey you, Stratos, yes, you, Stratos,*
> *fix us a fine narghilé!*
>
> *So Batis can have a smoke,*
> *who's been a head for years,*
> *and Artemis can smoke too,*
> *who travels and brings us back dope.*
>
> *He sends us Istanbul hashish*
> *and all of us get high,*
> *and fine Persian tobacco*
> *for the mangas to smoke in peace.*

Artemis had started to write songs too; he was the only member of the quartet with any musical training, and might have become one of the best known rembetika song-writers of all, but he had already started on his sad way down. In a brothel in Piraeus he had met a woman called Skoularikiou who was a drug addict. She soon turned him on to heroin, and he never got off it. Around 1934 he wrote one of the saddest of all rembetika songs, 'The Junkie's Complaint':

> *From the time I started to smoke the dose*
> *the world turned its back, I'm at a loss.*
>
> *Wherever I am people bother me,*
> *I can't bear to be called a junkie.*
>
> *From sniffing it up I went on the needle*
> *and slowly my body wasted away.*

Nothing was left to do in this world,
for dope led me to die in the streets.

Nine years later, on a cold winter's morning, Artemis was found lying dead on the street outside the teké Seraphim with his bouzouki clutched in his arms. He was twenty-nine years old. The few songs he had written were all to become rembetika classics — 'Poser', 'Crazy Nick', 'In the Hamam of Constantinople' (also called 'The Harem in the Hamam').

When the four friends, calling themselves the 'Tetras Xakousti' or 'Famous Quartet', began playing in a café in Piraeus, they were surprised at the crowds who came to listen to them. The music seemed to excite the audience, and there were fights nearly every night. Knives were used more than once, the police were called and crockery was broken. Tired of the fights, Markos decided to open a café of his own. This time he had with him the composer Kostas Skarvelis, who wrote a number of fine rembetika songs, including 'What does your mother tell you about me' and 'The sorrow in my heart'. But again there was trouble. The police refused to give Markos a permit unless he gave them information about hashish smokers, so the place closed down, and Markos took Batis and Yiorgos Rovertakis with him on a tour of his own island of Syros. It was after this trip that he wrote the most famous of all *hasapiko's*: 'Frankosyriani'.

By the time Markos and Stratos made their first recordings, Markos had written fifty or sixty songs, but his first song on record was 'You should have come with me, mangas, to our teké'. He had never thought of himself as a singer, and when he was invited to make a recording for Columbia, he intended them to use another singer while he played bouzouki, but he was persuaded to try singing himself and the result was that his deep, rasping voice became identified with the rembetika style, and other singers began to imitate it.

Despite his recognition as a musician, Markos was going through a difficult period of his life. His wife had had an affair with his best friend, Markos's knife-carrying brother attacked her, and there were violent quarrels between the two brothers. Although Markos knew he should leave his wife, he was still in love with her, and when they did eventually part he kept going back to spend a night with her, or just to stand under her window imagining her in bed with other men. It was at this time that he wrote the song 'Misbehaver' ('I don't want you, I don't want you, I don't love you any more').

He travelled around the countryside to get away from Athens, again with Batis, but this time in the company of another musician who was to become a legendary name in the rembetika — the great Yiannis Papaioannou, known as 'the Tall', a great lanky fellow with a beaky nose and a crazy grin. When they returned to Athens they began working together at a club in the suburb of Votanikos. This club, belonging to Vlachos, and another café nearby became the centre of rembetika music in the immediate pre-war years. The small group was expanded to an orchestra, with a santouri player and several female singers. From 1936-9 they played nightly and people from all classes of Athenian society, men and women, began going to listen to music which had come from the tekédhes of Piraeus, and which had now become fashionable entertainment.

The days of the tekédhes were almost over. During the war there was some relaxation of the laws against hashish, but the severe prosecutions of the Metaxas dictatorship (1936-41) had forced a lot of the tekédhes to close, and many of the smokers as well as the musicians had fled to Thessaloniki where conditions were somewhat easier. The local police chief there, Vassilis Mouskhoundis, was a rembetika fan, and was prepared to supply musicians with hashish in order to listen to them play the bouzoukia. Mouskhoundis became so popular with rembetika musicians that he acted as best-man at the wedding of composer Tsitsanis, who claimed that it was he who had advised the composer to take the rembetika out of the hashish dens and make the songs lighter. The recording companies were no longer allowed to make recordings of hashish songs, so the rembetika composers, at least for the time being, stopped composing them.[1] A new type of rembetika was about to become popular, and a new group of names to become famous, but before we move to the rembetika of the 40s and 50s it is time to look more closely at some of the characteristics

[1] Strict censorship of rembetika lyrics was apparently not introduced until 1937 (see Pennanen, 2004, pp. 11–12).

of pre-war rembetika, and the society which it reflected. For it was pre-war rembetika which established the style of rembetika music, and pre-war mangas society which gave it its framework. After the war there would be developments, mutations and an eventual disintegration of the rembetika, but subsequent changes were mostly based on the rembetika of the 1930s.

Papaioannou with the well-known Piraeus character Captain Andreas Zepos.

Piraeus in the 30s. A family outing for Apokreas, the Greek pre-Lenten carnival, when it is customary to wear fancy dress. The man on the right is playing a bouzouki.

4

Rembetika high — Smyrna style and Piraeus style

Markos Vamvakaris was only one of a number of important pre-war rembetika musicians. I've concentrated on him because he was a representative figure of his time — he not only played the music; he lived the life of a rembetis. And it is always more interesting to get to know one man a little than to be presented with a lot of names to which there is not enough space to attach faces. Now it is time to say a little about other musicians and about the sort of music which existed on the periphery of the rembetika.

I said that the so-called Smyrna style, which many Asia Minor refugees favoured, was different in character and instrumentation to the Piraeus rembetika of Markos and his friends. By the Second World War the Smyrna style had almost disappeared, but some of its major characteristics had been absorbed into the rembetika. Not only were the modes and rhythms of the Smyrna style common, but female singers who were important artists in the cafés aman began to perform with rembetika musicians, paving the way for such partnerships as that between Vassilis Tsitsanis and Marika Ninou.

The two styles of the teké and the café might have continued to co-exist without cohabiting if it had not been for the publicity which the recording studios trained on the rembetika. When the voices of Markos, Stratos and Papaioannou became familiar to people all over Greece, rembetes were winkled out of the tekédhes and caves of Piraeus into the cafés and night-clubs of Athens. At the same time, the police of the Metaxas dictatorship were cracking down severely on hashish smokers, and the old quarter of Piraeus where many of them lived was torn down.

In Athens, the refugees had already established numerous cafés where women as well as men could listen to music. Some of the cafés where rembetika musicians began performing were owned by Asia Minor refugees. These cafés had also set a taste for larger groups of players and a variety of instruments. As the bouzouki players moved into the cafés and clubs, they looked for pianists, guitarists and accordion players to fill out their ensembles. They also began to attract the already-established singers of the cafés, male and female, to the rembetika clubs. All this happened towards the end of the pre-war period. The new style of rembetika which emerged only really established itself after 1940. Before then it is possible to separate the two styles of Piraeus rembetika music and Asia Minor style café music, and to examine their characteristics.

I've already said something about the music of the café aman. In Athens, as the refugees opened up cafés around the outer suburbs, the music they played was very much what they would have played in Smyrna or Istanbul. There were long improvised pieces for violin, santouri or voice — oriental-sounding melodies, often unaccompanied or briefly supported by an instrument which kept the rhythm and doubled occasionally at the octave. There were also Greek and Turkish folk songs and other popular songs including some that were about the same subjects as the rembetika. Composers like Panayiotis Toundas, Evangelos Papazoglou, Yiannis Dragatsis, Kostas Skarvelis, Kostas Tzovenos and Spyros Peristeris, all of whom wrote and performed in café aman style, also composed songs that referred to the underworld and the hashish-smoking manges. Instrumentalists like Kostas Kanoulas, the cellist and cimbalom-player, Agapios Tomboulis, who played the outi and the çümbüş (a banjo-like instrument), and Dimitrios Semsis, the violinist, were virtuosos whose technique was greatly admired. Singers like Kostas Roukounas from Samos, Andonis Dalgas, Marika Politissa, Rita Abatzi and Rosa Eskenazi were all so popular that songs came to be associated with them as performers. The singers, like the instrumentalists, performed unaccompanied, improvised solos, using the modes or *maqams* of late Ottoman music, and a florid voice style.

The music which was sung and played in these cafés of the late 20s and early 30s may have belonged largely to an oral tradition which went far back into the 19th century, but the musicians who set up the Association of Athenian and Piraeus Musicians, with its headquarters in the Mikrasia café, in 1928, were accomplished professionals. When they were called on to play in any one of the new styles becoming fashionable in Athens, they were capable of adapting their techniques to the new tastes. When they arrived in Athens, the Smyrna musicians found there was already a love of Italianate serenades which had filtered into Greece via the Ionian islands. These *kantadhes* were usually sung by groups of men and women in western harmony accompanied by mandolins or guitars. Their simple, romantic melodies no doubt influenced the rembetika song-writers, if less so than the more oriental style of the refugees. The Europeanizing process was accelerated by the spread of radio, and with it the fashion for European dance music of the period, particularly the fox-trot and tango.

The Smyrna musicians were no slower in adapting to the new fashion for the rembetika than they were in catering to the taste for European dance music. Once rembetika music began to be played on the radio and in cafés, singers like Roukounas and Rosa Eskenazi began recording rembetika songs, the pianist Rovertakis played rembetika music on the piano, the guitarist Vangelis Papazoglou and the saz-player Iovan Tsaous both began to play and write write rembetika songs, and a number of instrumentalists, who saw which way the wind was blowing, took up the bouzouki.

The rembetika players who had grown up in the streets and tekédhes of Piraeus were not always welcome in the smarter cafés of Athens, despite their popularity with the public. Yiorgos Rovertakis, the Smyrna-born pianist who had been playing in cafés around Athens since 1925, describes Papaioannou's attempt to get a job at the café Tzitzifies, and the manager's unwillingness to employ him because he was known as a hashish-smoker. But whether or not they understood or cared for rembetika players, the rembetika were so popular by the mid-30s that club owners had to employ them. Pikinos's place at Thission, Vlachos's at Votanikos, 'Serelia' at Omonia where Rosa was singing — these musical cafés were full of Athenians, and Athenians wanted to hear bouzoukis and the rembetika. A new style of rembetika, catering to a wider, more bourgeois public, was about to be established. But before looking at the new style, what were the main characteristics of the old?

First of all, Piraeus rembetika was almost exclusively male music. It was sung by men, played by men, danced to by men, and generally listened to by men. By the Second World War this had changed, but during the 20s and most of the 30s female singers stayed within the café aman, or Smyrna style. In the early rembetika, the taximia, the long improvised pieces familiar to Arabic and Turkish music, were an important introduction to the songs. They set the mood of the song and allowed the performer, usually high on hashish, to wander in controlled fantasy. The taximia were played with great emotional involvement — often with great technical skill too, although they were never mere vehicles for displays of virtuosity. The bouzouki or baglama player was turning himself and his audience on. The taximi was sometimes followed by a brief rhythmical introduction, and then the song. As the rembetika performers began making recordings, the taximia were pruned to a brief introduction and sometimes omitted entirely. The three minute playing time of a 78 r.p.m. record had already dictated an important change in style.

In chapter six, I will deal in more detail with the modal types of rembetika songs, but it is important to realize that the scales used in the rembetika, like those which occur in oriental music, Greek Orthodox church music and a lot of Greek folk music, cannot be neatly categorized as major and minor. They are not, strictly speaking, scales at all. Scales are progressions of notes going straight up and down. The modal types or 'roads' of the rembetika are written out as scales in a number of sources, but this is misleading, in that each mode is characterized by certain melodic patterns, dominant notes, and intervals. The taximi's function was partly to establish the mood and character of the mode and partly to display the player's skill in improvising in the tradition. Although later rembetika songs were often composed in western minor and major keys, they continued to use characteristic melodic phrases from the earlier tradition of modes. Greek musicians of the Piraeus style used Turkish names for the modes they played in, but not always to refer to the equivalent mode. Few of them had any formal training in Ottoman Turkish music, and their terminology for the 'roads' they used varied from musician to musician.

One of the difficulties of combining other instruments with the bouzouki, or even of using two bouzoukis as 'primo' and 'secondo', was the fact that the melodies of the early rembetika, like those of Turkish music, were from a monophonic tradition; they did not 'fit' with European harmony based on the major and minor scales. The earliest rembetika songs were accompanied by a single instrumentalist, usually playing the melody, or striking the open strings, which were tuned in fifths.

As the taste for western-style harmony and large ensembles developed, rembetika players began using a small number of basic chords with their melodies, but despite a gradual westernization and hybridization of the music, rembetika musicians continued to use the old modes, combining them in creative ways with chordal harmony.

Many of the melodies of the early rembetika were borrowed from older folk melodies, both Turkish and Greek, and when the rembetika composers began inventing their own tunes, they were usually simple melodies with characteristic patterns of ornamentation. Frequently they consisted of a pair of melodic phrases, each half being repeated twice, with an introductory phrase recurring between the verses. What makes the songs musically interesting is a combination of factors: the half-oriental, half-occidental sounding melody, the insistent rhythm, especially the oddly attractive 9/8 rhythm of the zebekiko, the contrast between the bouncing rhythm and bright timbre of the bouzouki and the sour-sad lyrics, and above all the quality of the singer's voice, which may be nasal, grating, or metallic, but is never sweet. It retains just enough oriental colouring to give it emotional force, and just enough of the crudity of Piraeus speech to save it from sentimentality. Even without understanding a word of Greek, you can feel the swagger and the flair of the manges in pre-war rembetika songs.

It is this quality of flair, this posture of defiance in the face of poverty, repression and even death, which seems to me the most attractive feature of mangas society. As the lyrics of the rembetika songs and the descriptions of the rembetika musicians depict them, the manges were far from being the idealistic, daring young braves a number of modern Greek writers would have us believe. They were, however, members of an extremely interesting sub-culture, whose beliefs and habits remain in a rare state of preservation thanks to the words of the rembetika songs.

The defiant posture of the manges was, naturally enough, most obvious in their attitude to the police. It is not so much that they protest their ill-treatment: in fact they feel some pride in having 'eaten wood' (been beaten up) and served their time in jail; it is rather a refusal to change their way of life or to be submissive before the police, or to lose their sense of humour. 'Mr Policeman, don't beat us,' say the two pickpockets in Papazoglou's song 'The Pickpockets', of 1933, 'because you know very well that this is our job. And don't expect a kick-back. We pinch wallets and purses so the jail doors can see us nice and regular inside. Death doesn't scare us, it's only the hunger we mind; that's why we pick pockets and manage to have a swell time.'

A similar attitude is seen in 'The Handbag Snatcher', an amusing song of Petropouleas's, where the thief asks the policeman who is beating him to stop while he tells him the real story of how he stole a lady's handbag as she was getting into a taxi. At the end of the song he offers the policeman a sizeable bribe to release him.

It is not only towards the police that the manges are contemptuous. The bourgeois society, with its emphasis on money and its inability to enjoy itself, is frequently the butt of rembetika humour, as in this song of Markos's:

> Bouzouki, joy of the world, which entertained the manges,
> even the rich play a big trick on you now.

> They put you on their carpets, and in their smart front rooms,
> higher than the violin, friend, two steps further up.

> You went up in a lift, into their blocks of flats;
> and you played and they enjoyed you, those spoilt society brats.

> Now you'll go up even higher, as high as the planet Mars,
> even to the great Apollo, and he'll enjoy you too.

There is an unmistakable flavour of swagger about these lyrics, of pride in being on the outside, which was emphasized by the manges in their style of dress.

A mangas fashion-plate: Mathesis in a 'republican' and spats.

The history of bizarre and extravagant dressing in the Greek underworld goes back to the koutsavakidhes, the forerunners of the manges, whose brushes with the police were often occasioned by their deliberately provocative clothes. When Baraktaris, the Athens Chief of Police, caught koutsavakidhes wearing their jackets with an arm in one sleeve only, he would order the empty sleeve to be cut off.

Markos, whose mother's family were tailors, had heard descriptions of the elaborate, expensive suits ordered by the koutsavakidhes of Syros a generation before. He himself listed his four passions in life as flowers, book-learning, music and clothes. In his day, the manges fancied Borsalino 'republicans', English-style suits, carefully groomed moustaches and slicked-down hair; but even these accoutrements were worn with an eccentric disregard for convention. Markos insisted on wearing a singlet and working-man's cap together with his smart English suit instead of the regulation tie and 'republican'.

Just as the manges complained to the police who abused them without really expecting mercy, their attitude to death was a mixture of defiance and resignation. Many rembetika songs which refer to death in the guise of Charos, the traditional Greek folk personification, invoke him in familiar conversation. The finest of these Charos songs have a quality of shock about them. The confrontation between death and the mangas character is so vivid and personal that Charos comes uncomfortably close:

> In the mountains of Pendeli, oh mother, I walk among the pines
> and look for Death although he is a stranger.

> In the mountains of Pendeli, oh mother, one sweet break of day
> we meet at last and painfully I speak:

> 'Leave me time to live, Death — I have a wife,' I say,
> 'and children too, oh mother, and don't know how to leave them.'

> He sees me and smiles, oh mother, and I start to fade away;
> in a loud voice he says: 'I take you, I don't leave you.'

A song which appears in a number of different versions describes a meeting between Death and a group of hashish-smokers. They enquire how their comrades are getting on down below, and at the end of the song ask Charos to take some hashish to their deprived colleagues in the underworld.

The manges claimed to be non-violent, and yet most carried knives and many were involved in serious fights. There was probably some truth to their claims that they were not looking for trouble, but violence was a feature of the underworld which they had to be prepared for. Knives were the common weapon of the streets and were used in café fights. These fights usually followed heavy drinking sessions, and may have been one reason why many manges preferred to frequent the tekédhes, where violence was rare. One of the most serious fights to take place in the rembetika world was in 1931 at Pikinos's café, where Roukounas was singing. A noisy, drunken group of customers pestered the musicians until the owner remonstrated and was stabbed by one of the customers in the stomach. He later died in hospital, coughing over a cigarette which his brother smuggled in to him. The fine bouzouki player and composer, Mikhailis Yenitsaris, had a series of fights with the police, although he seems to have frequented the cafés rather than the tekédhes of Piraeus. Fights still occur in bouzouki clubs, sometimes over the right to dance a zebekiko. One such notorious case in the 1970s ended in the death of several patrons and became the subject of a popular song by Dionysis Savvopoulos[1] as well as of the film *Request*, directed by Nikos Koundouros. But the manges who smoked hashish did so to forget the rigors of their lives and to enjoy a little music. 'If I smoke hashish, I don't bother anyone,' as Tsitsanis said in 'The Dew'.

There is some ambiguity in the manges' attitude to violence. They admired toughness, but only when it was absolute. They were dandies, but they hated posturers. The song 'Poser' or 'Mangas, if you're going to use your knife' by Anestis Delias (1935) gives an indication of how such a 'false mangas' was regarded:

> *Mangas, if you're going to use your knife*
> *you'd better have the guts, poser, to take it out.*
>
> *That stuff doesn't wash with me, so hide your blade*
> *or I'll get high, poser, and come round to your shack.*
>
> *Go somewhere else, poser, and strut your stuff*
> *because I've been smoking, poser, and I'm mighty high.*

[1] Savvopoulos is an important contemporary Greek song-writer, as well known for his acerbic social commentary as for his music.

I told you to sit tight because I'll beat you up;
I'll come with my gun, poser, and I'll call your bluff.

In their attitudes to women, the manges were even more ambiguous than in their attitude to violence. They all seem to have had a number of mistresses, many of them whores. Wives, if they had them, were left at home to produce children and be maligned for complaining. The women the manges mixed with often had a measure of independence which was unusual in Greece. Living in a city, many of them worked, even if only as prostitutes, and were therefore in a position to leave their men or be unfaithful. The rembetika songs which are not simply adoring and romantic, paint a picture of women as torturers — jealous, cold and unfaithful. They are always 'burning' the hearts of their men. Markos's song 'Ah, you bitch' is typical...

Ah, you bitch, you've wounded me so much,
you make a slave of me with all your tricks.

You've made me crazy, sent me off my head,
I'll never get my heart back again.

Gypsies and oriental women, on the other hand, are pictured as warmer and more exotic, and some of those who were refugees from Asia Minor smoked hashish, which made them still more congenial. An old mangas friend of mine told me his grandmother had turned him on to hashish when he was a child. Mothers, too, escape censure. They are depicted as sacred, suffering and regretfully abandoned by their wayward sons.

There are other characteristics of mangas society which the rembetika songs reveal, such as conspicuous generosity, spontaneity, a certainty that the manges know how to enjoy themselves better than most other Greeks, a reliance on fate to control and excuse their actions. The manges formed a true sub-culture which felt itself to be outside the mainstream of society, and one of the charms of the rembetika is that the songs were both the creation and the mirror of this sub-culture. As the rembetika music which they created became popular with the mainstream of Greek society, it lost its power to represent the manges. The rembetika of the 40s and 50s was still in touch with the society of the manges, but it had taken an important step away from them, and it was already beginning to look back with nostalgia to the world of the Piraeus tekédhes.

Narghilé.

Greek women partisans during the Second World War: cover of a partisan newspaper called 'Fighters for Freedom'.

5

The Indian summer of the rembetika: the war years and Tsitsanis

For some reason, there seems to have been less publicity about the sufferings of the Greeks during the Second World War than about other Europeans. During the years of the Italian and then the German occupation, not only did almost the entire Jewish population of Greece perish, but hundreds of thousands of Greeks died of starvation. In Athens, in the terrible winter of 1940–41, hundreds of bodies were found in the streets each morning, and hunger continued through the barbarous days of the civil war which followed. The only force which held Greece together during the war seemed to be the partisan movement E.A.M. (National Liberation Front), with its rebel army E.L.A.S. (National Popular Liberation Army), which operated in the mountains of Greece, harrying the Germans and giving Greeks some vestige of pride and self-respect. The civil war was in many ways much more damaging to the country's morale. The interference of the British and later American governments, combined with the rigidity and brutality of the leaders of the Communist Party of Greece, the K.K.E., led to a bloody, treacherous conflict the effects of which lasted almost to the end of the 20th century. As usual, it was the *kosma-ki*, the poor people, who suffered most during the war years, but they were joined by a large number of students, intellectuals and some political leaders. The witch-hunting of communists, which had been lively enough during Metaxas's pre-war, fascist-leaning dictatorship, became open warfare. By the time the communists were finally defeated, with all the latest American equipment trained against them including napalm, the prisons overflowed with political prisoners and the now familiar prison islands, such as Ikaria and Makronissos, became vast camps of torture and degradation.

During these nightmare years, many rembetika musicians died, including Kostas Skarvelis and Panayiotis Toundas. Those who could find work continued to perform. New clubs were opened and new songs written. It would be an exaggeration to say that rembetika musicians were active in the resistance. Some, like Sotiria Bellou, who joined the partisans, were; most were not. And yet the rembetes were not indifferent to the sufferings which went on around them, and a number of songs were written during the war and the civil war which commented directly or indirectly on the situation. What was more important was that rembetika songs, often written before the war, were sung all over the country by a population which felt them to be an expression of their collective suffering and anger.

In the 1970s, I met an old second-hand bookseller in Athens who had spent years in a German prison camp. He knew that I was looking for material about the rembetika and he said that he had never thought much about the music before the war, or listened to the words of the songs, but when he was in the prison camp, a mangas prisoner had begun singing a rembetika song. He said, 'You know, the words were quite ordinary...nothing to do with the war, but when he began singing, we all knew he was saying something for us, defying the guards, and it gave us heart.'

Songs dealing directly with the war were rare. Yenitsaris's 'Saltadoros', describing how he and his mangas friends would leap on the backs of German trucks and steal the spare jerry-cans of petrol and kerosene to sell on the black market, was written in 1942, but for obvious reasons not recorded until long afterwards. Stratos's 'How many hearts wept?' came out in 1946, but referred specifically to the occupation, and to the profits made by many of the Greek bourgeoisie out of the German black market:

> How many hearts wept in those black years
> that we lived in slavery, treated like dirt?
>
> How many young bodies and lives were wiped out?
> How many homes shut forever for this crime?
>
> The German black market caused it all;
> it forced our people into misery.

Let them see, those who made our hearts burn,
and got rich and enjoyed themselves on our despair.

Another song written at the end of the war was Roukounas's 'The Bomb':

Over there in America
a new bomb has just come out.

One they've dropped on Japan,
and destroyed the whole society.

Two songs which were less explicit became so popular during the civil war period that they were banned. One was Kaldaras's 'Night without moon':

Night without moon, the darkness is deep,
yet a brave young lad cannot sleep.

What is he waiting for, all night long,
at the narrow window that lights his cell?

The door opens and shuts but it's double-locked.
What's the boy done that they've thrown him in jail?

The door opens and shuts with a heavy sigh.
If only I could guess the sorrow of his heart.

The other song was Tsitsanis's 'Some mother sighs', which describes a mother waiting patiently for her boy to return from 'the black foreign land'.

Tsitsanis's 'Cloudy Sunday', one of the most famous of all rembetika songs, was not released on record until 1948, but Tsitsanis had written it during the Occupation, and its gloomy nostalgia was to become characteristic of many of the composer's post-war songs...

Cloudy Sunday, you look like my heart
which is always cloudy, Christ and the Virgin.

You're a day like the one when I lost my joy.
Cloudy Sunday, you make my heart bleed!

When I see you rainy, I can't find peace,
you make my life black, and I heave a deep sigh.

During the war years in Athens and Thessaloniki, a number of the bouzouki clubs and cafés which had flourished in the late 1930s were still popular, even if they were now frequented by German officers and their Greek girlfriends. The clubs at Votanikos were closed, but performers like Markos, Keromitis and Papaioannou all found work at clubs like Dalezio's at Omonia, the Hotel Kostala, and the Karé tou Assou. The record companies had shut down though, and it was not until 1947 that the rembetika recovered its vitality.

From 1946 until about 1952, there was an Indian summer of the rembetika, a burst of creativity and popularity which centred around a young man who was already an accomplished rembetika musician before the war, and who became, by the 50s, the best-known name in the history of the rembetika.

Vassilis Tsitsanis was very different from the pre-war rembetika composers. Although he mixed with the rembetes, and frequented

A new star rises: Vassilis Tsitsanis, king of the new rembetika.

the tekédhes, he was not from the usual mangas background. Son of a poor shoe-maker, he was born in Trikala, in central north Greece, in 1915. When he came to Athens to enrol at Athens University, he was already playing the bouzouki and he soon abandoned his studies to be a full-time performer and composer. From 1938–40 he left Athens to do his military service in Thessaloniki, but he continued to write songs at an amazing rate. Despite a popularity which bordered on idolatry, he remained a shy, reserved man, who wore quietly expensive English sports jackets as if he belonged in them, and smiled with sad Byzantine eyes at his enthusiastic audiences.

Tsitsanis's first recording, in 1937, was the song 'This is why I wander the streets of Athens'. By 1940 he had recorded a hundred songs, most of them his own compositions. In these early recordings his style was very similar to Markos's, and he used Stratos to perform several of them. After the war he began to experiment with a broader variety of styles, and to use female vocalists. His first female singer was Daisy Stavropoulou, a young girl who was only fifteen years old at the time, and had a voice which was curiously similar to Stratos's. So much so that Stratos complained to Tsitsanis: 'That girl's stolen all my tricks.' But it was not until he discovered Sotiria Bellou that Tsitsanis found an ideal female singer for his songs. Bellou could be thought of as the Bessie Smith of the rembetika. She was jailed (ostensibly for attacking her husband with vitriol, but the authorities may have used this excuse because of her known left-wing sympathies), and vilified for her lesbian relationships. She was never a crowd-pleaser, and by the 1970s she looked undeniably severe, sitting on a hard-backed chair on the platform with her ankles neatly crossed and her hair cropped off like the botany mistress at a girls' private school. And yet Bellou quietly helped a number of young musicians who were hard up, and all the musicians who knew her well liked her. She had, I believe, the greatest voice of any rembetika singer.

Bellou was not exactly Tsitsanis's discovery. The playwright Kapitanakis, a fan of the rembetika, heard her singing in an Athens taverna and introduced her to him, but once Tsitsanis heard her sing, she was on her way to stardom. For the next two years she made recordings with Tsitsanis while he wrote song after song in the new style which was partly his own and partly influenced by the popular songs from Europe which were flowing into Greece. Most of the songs he wrote at this time were love songs. Hashish songs and prison songs were less common in the repertoire of the rembetika after the war, and even songs dealing with the life of the manges seemed like nostalgic revivals of a world which no longer existed. Tsitsanis's lyrics were generally softer, more pleading than those of the pre-war composers. A typical example is 'Take off your mask'...

> *For me you will always remain a stranger,*
> *false woman, false heart.*
>
> *Take off your mask so that I can know you,*
> *let's get things straight this evening.*

...or the song 'Make up a bed for me to sleep'...

> *I took the road and I've come*
> *through the rain, and got soaked,*
> *and at your steps I whistle.*
> *Open up and let me come inside*
> *and make up a bed for me to sleep.*

The rembetika was now public, respectable entertainment. The clubs of the period, Tzitzifies, Jimmy the Fat's, Rossignol, Triana, all had large groups of players and singers, some of whom, like Papaioannou, Hadzichristou, Keromitis and Markos, had made their names before the war, others who were relatively unknown — Hiotis, Tsaousakis, Bellou, and Marika Nikolaidou, better known as Ninou, who was to be Tsitsanis's second successful female singer. She began singing with him at Jimmy the Fat's and continued making recordings with him until 1953 when she left for America. Whereas Bellou's voice had the power and bite to transform what might have been

⟶ *Tzitzifies in 1948: the Kalamata group, one of the most famous teams of rembetika musicians ever to play together. They include Markos, centre of middle row, with his brother on his right and the guitarist Kostas Roukounas, the 'Samiot,' on his far left, and in the front row, left to right, Keromitis, Hadzichristou, Mitsakis, Papaioannou and Manisalis.*

Tsitsanis and Ninou in 1950.

sentimental songs into bitterly tragic ones, Ninou's voice was light and feminine. Tsitsanis wisely made use of her lilting, sensuous, café-aman style voice for some of his gayer songs like 'The Little Crabs'.

Markos, Papaioannou and Stratos continued performing the old rembetika they had known before the war, but fashions had changed, and Stratos and Papaioannou both adjusted to the new conditions. Stratos recorded a number of Tsitsanis's songs, and Papaioannou, who was a born entertainer, attracted new audiences with his gangling charm and a grin like an insane skeleton. He wasn't slow to recognize the extraordinary quality of Sotiria Bellou's voice, and soon used her to record some of his best post-war songs, including the famous '*Anixé, anixé, yiati dhen andeho*' — 'Open up, I can't bear it any more'. He also performed and recorded with Ninou, Tsitsanis, and the leading musicians of his day.

The better-known performers of the period moved about from club to club and toured the countryside. New records of rembetika songs were being made at an astonishing rate, and as the country began slowly to recover from the disastrous years of war and civil war, the bouzouki clubs became increasingly popular, luxurious and expensive. A handful of musicians and musicologists showed an interest in the rembetika for the first time, and Hadzidakis's and Theodorakis's interest was to be important in the development of Greek popular music.

Had it not been for Tsitsanis, I doubt if the rembetika would ever have recovered its pre-war popularity. Even Papaioannou remained popular with a narrower audience, most of whom were already interested in the rembetika before the war, and Markos was no longer fashionable. Tsitsanis took the rembetika across class and urban associations into the open field of popular music. His songs are still rembetika in style, although the melodies tend towards major and minor rather than the old roads, and his lyrics are generally more romantic, less socially oriented than the songs of the 30s. The singing stars of the period, especially the amazing Bellou and the big, acid-voiced Tsaousakis, added a new dimension to the songs, and the fuller orchestration appealed to a broader public.

It was in the late 1950s that the rembetika took a downward turn from which they never quite recov-

Papaioannou with his son.

ered. The mid-50s saw the emergence of the *archondorembetes* — the rembetika musicians who really got rich. Mostly they were bouzouki players with impressive techniques and the showmanship to exploit them. The earliest, and probably the greatest virtuoso of the bouzouki, was Manolis Hiotis. He had begun playing before the war, but he only emerged as a star in the 1950s, particularly after he added a fourth string to his bouzouki and changed the tuning, enabling him to play faster, and to supply full guitar-like accompaniments. He was soon followed by the great majority of bouzouki players. The electrification of the bouzouki completed the transformation. What had been a delicate, lightly-strung, undecorated instrument that could be played with a fingernail, became as vulgar a piece of pop art as you could wish to see. Inlaid with mother-of-pearl, amplified to a literally deafening pitch and accompanied by the ubiquitous electric organ, the bouzouki had become Greece's answer to the electric guitar.

The bourgeois minority who had begun going to hear the rembetika before the war swelled to a majority in the clubs of the late 1950s and early 1960s. It became not only fashionable to go 'to the bouzoukis', as it began to be called, but prohibitively expensive. Audiences before the war had often become excited, especially when there was a good dancer on the floor. Now the excitement was extravagantly displayed. Plates and glasses were thrown at the feet of the dancer, and customers were happily overcharged for the breakages. The style of dancing had also undergone a marked change. The hasapiko, or butchers' dance, which was performed by pairs or occasionally a group of three male dancers, had been danced with a minimum of movement. It was a precise, smooth dance, the attraction of which lay in the synchronized footwork of the dancers. Now that so much attention was trained on the dancers, young men began introducing new, flashy patterns of steps, which they would practise together for hours. It looked good, and the budding tourist trade liked to watch it. The faster *hasaposerviko* — or Serbian style hasapiko, a common Balkan dance — was revived in the 60s for similar reasons.

The zebekiko suffered a similar fate to the hasapiko. It had been an introspective improvised dance. It was danced with restrained but evident emotion. In the late 50s and early 60s, the zebekiko became studiedly dramatic. It also became acrobatic. There were leaps and twists in mid-air, and slappings of the shoes. It was often skilful and attractive to watch, but it was a new dance, and the customers went on smashing their specially ordered piles of plates in ritual displays of appreciation.

It became impossible to drink barrelled wine or eat cheap food in the clubs, but this was one of the attractions for the bourgeoisie. They ordered whiskey or expensive imported wine, ate over-priced, inferior food, and broke plates in competitive displays of extravagance. Working-class Greeks, still enthusiastic to hear the rembetika and unable to afford the clubs regularly, saved up for months to spend a month's wages on a night at the bouzoukis. The manges had always been extravagant and reckless with money when they had any, and it was perhaps a hangover from their improvidence which caused the Greeks who could least afford it to squander money on a night's music. Thousands of drachmas would often be thrown at the virtuoso bouzouki players, who were already earning princely sums. Zambetas became the self-styled king of bouzouki, and the archondorembetes were raking in the drachmas. All the bouzouki clubs had female singers, most of whom had big sexy voices and chests to match. They

*Tsitsanis and Bellou performing together in the 1970s, with rembetophile
Kostas Hadzidoulis.*

also had a sort of uniform of tight shiny dresses with a lot of glitter
and spangles, bracelets that clinked, and gold earrings that glinted.
They were the *bouzoukloudhes*, an up-to-date version of the old café
aman singers, and they provided a sort of kewpie-doll eroticism in the
clubs.

It was still possible, in the late 50s and early 60s, to hear good rembetika music in some of the clubs. Bellou, Tsaousakis, Papaioannou
and Stratos all opened their own clubs, where they continued to perform 30s and 40s style rembetika with only a moderate concession to
modern orchestration and amplification tastes. But they were not the
most successful stars of the period. Public taste had moved away from
the rembetika to the related but transformed style of popular music
being performed by such stars as Zambetas, Marinella, and Kazantzides. Tsitsanis had begun the trend towards a broader-based style of
popular music which was to go a long way further and prepare the
ground for the development of popular music composed by the classically-trained Theodorakis and Hadzidakis. Both of these composers
made use of rembetika rhythms, instruments, singers and performers

in their music. Hadzidakis had been interested in the rembetika since the 40s. Theodorakis's interest came later, and he learned much of what he knew from Hiotis, but the result was a new and exciting style of popular music.

The word laïki, which means folk or popular, had begun to be applied to all kinds of Greek city music including the rembetika, to distinguish it from dhimotiki, or village music. As the rembetika became more Europeanized, and city composers began writing popular songs with European-sounding melodies and rembetika rhythms, the line between the styles became blurred, and laïki was a useful generalization. In fact the rembetika which this book is about was a historical phenomenon by the end of the 50s, although it survived in a few corners of Athens until the mid-60s.

During the 1967–74 dictatorship there was a revival of interest in the older-style rembetika, but many of the big figures of the pre-war rembetika were dead. The re-mastering of early rembetika records helped foster an interest in the music among young Greeks, many of whom took up the bouzouki or baglama and began forming rembetika ensembles. Among popular composers, the influence of the rembetika continued to be strong, and Dionysis Savvopoulos, one the most original song-writers of the 1970s, esteemed by both young students and intellectuals, used Sotiria Bellou to sing a memorable zebekiko he had composed. What seemed to be a sudden fad for the older rembetika continued to grow in the last decades of the 20th century, as the rembetika was embraced not only by young Greeks and visitors to Greece but by performers and listeners all over the world. Removed from its original context, the music was adopted by Greek politicians and cultural leaders as the quintessence of Greekness. Beyond Greece, it appealed to the newly-emerging market for urban folk music and 'World Music'. Today it occupies a position analogous to tango in Argentina or flamenco in Spain. The once-despised music of the Piraeus underworld has become an instantly recognizable national symbol.

6

The bones of the rembetika:
roads and modes

By the 1950s, Greeks no longer talked of going to listen to the rembetika, but of going 'sta bouzoukia' — to the bouzoukis. This emphasis on the instrument rather than the singer coincided with the rise of the virtuoso bouzouki players like Manolis Hiotis, whose technique was legendary. By this time many players were playing eight-stringed (i.e. four pairs of strings) bouzoukis, tuned like a guitar. The extra two strings facilitated the playing of rapid passages and encouraged the use of chordal style which was foreign to the rembetika.

I remember a conversation I once had with Paco Peña, the flamenco guitarist whom many Spaniards then considered to be the greatest living virtuoso on the instrument. He said he was glad that the flamenco guitar had become a virtuoso solo instrument because he loved it and earned his living by it, but in some ways he thought it was bad for flamenco. 'In flamenco,' he said, 'the singer comes first, then the dancer, and then the guitar.' He went on to say that he never played the guitar in Spain for his friends unless someone felt moved to dance or sing.

The rembetika seem to me to be similarly integrated as a form. The songs are, without exception, written in dance rhythms. This is not to say that they must be danced, but the three elements of song, dance rhythm and instrumental accompaniment are always present.

The music

The rembetika developed in the towns and particularly the ports of Greece at a time when the Turks still occupied large areas of the country and a considerable proportion of the Greek population lived in what

75

is now Turkey where Turkish music had been played alongside Greek folk music for centuries. The Greeks were, at least at the time when I was first interested in the rembetika, anxious to play down the extent of the Turkish influence on the rembetika or on any other form of Greek music. If they admitted there was a Turkish element in the music, they said that the Turks borrowed their music from the Byzantines. Certainly the interdependence of eastern-Greek and western-Turkish music is high. The musical terminology of the rembetika is Turkish, not surprisingly because it developed in the late Ottoman Empire where the dominant musical tradition had a vocabulary for such things as modal types and tunings. It is significant that the flourishing of the rembetika as a popular form of music followed closely on the Turko-Greek War of 1920–22 and the consequent influx of Asia Minor refugees, many of whom were only 'Greek' by virtue of their religion, into mainland Greece. Many of the early rembetika musicians were either from Asia Minor or from the islands close to the Turkish coast. In the cosmopolitan centres they came from, such as Smyrna, there was an eclectic mixture of languages and musical styles.

Perhaps it is enough to say about the musical origins of the rembetika that the melodies conform to modal types which occur in Greek folk music, Byzantine church music, Turkish folk music and Turkish classical music. The rhythms are similarly interwoven, but it is worth noting that the most common rhythm of the rembetika, the 9/8 of the zebekiko, is unusual in Greek or Turkish music from any other region except the western coast of Turkey and the islands off the Turkish coast such as Mytilini (Lesbos).

Turkish elements are more apparent in the early rembetika and the music of the café aman, with its *koumpania* of demotic instruments and its 'alla Turca' singers. The unaccompanied vocal solo known in Turkish as gazel, in Greek as amané, was among the favourite types of music performed in these cafés, and a number of the early rembetika musicians recorded such songs. Roukounas wrote a number of verses for amanédhes and he and Stratos Payioumdzis also recorded them. Conversely, many of the musicians who are thought of as café aman-style performers rather than rembetika musicians and who recorded mostly songs in the Asia Minor style, also recorded rembetika songs.

Among the professional Smyrna-style singers, who not only recorded songs of low life but specifically songs about hashish-smoking, were Rosa Eskenazi, Rita Abatzi, Marika Politissa, Andonis Dalgas, and Stellakis Perpiniades. In fact, the performers and styles were so interwoven, especially in the pre-Second World War period, that it is difficult to make a clear division between them.

As the rembetika became more popular and more firmly centred in the Piraeus-Athens area, they were increasingly exposed to western European influences. The diffusion of European dance-band music and the popularity of the Neapolitan-sounding kantadhes, which had come to Athens via the Ionian islands, affected the rembetika in a number of ways. Melodies, instruments and words were borrowed from the West. The guitar became popular, along with the piano and the accordion. Western harmony suitable to such instruments came to be expected and as rembetika musicians formed themselves into groups, they began supplying bass parts to their songs. This tended to pull the rembetika melodies out of their old modal types towards diatonic major and minor keys, but the melodic characteristics of the modal style remained a distinguishing trait of the rembetika through the post-war period. By the 1950s, it was possible for Tsitsanis to say: 'In the rembetika there are only major and minor scales.' It was not true, but major and minor harmonies were being regularly applied to rembetika melodies.

The roads

As I have pointed out, rembetika songs are based not on scales in the western sense of the word but on modal types which can be written out in the form of a scale yet which have characteristic phrases and patterns of movement. Certain notes are more important than others, certain relations between notes are stressed. In Ottoman music, there were dozens of these modes or maqams and each was felt to have a special character suited to a particular emotion, mood or time of day. Just as a classical Indian musician has a large number of modal types at his disposal from which he can choose a *rag* and build a complicated pattern of improvisation, so the Arab or Turkish musician has a repository of maqams. Having chosen one, he can then explore its possibilities in a *taxim*, or improvised piece.

Early rembetika musicians still used the word maqam for the modal types but they soon became known by the Greek word *dhromi* — literally roads. The word taxim acquired a Greek form taximi (plural taximia) and is still used to refer to the improvised introductions to rembetika songs where the instrumentalist explores the *dhromos*, road, in which the song is written.

A lot of extravagant claims have been made about the large number of roads used in the rembetika, but at least in the repertoire of the rembetika recorded in Greece after 1930 there were never more than a dozen roads in common use.

Thanassis Bastas, 'The Syrianos', playing an old bouzouki made about 1900. Thanassis was one of the few players able to teach his pupils the old 'roads' of rembetika.

The commonest roads were rast, *houzam, hijaz* and *hijazkar*, or *piraiotiko*, two closely related roads, both characterized by an interval of an augmented 2nd between the 2nd and 3rd degrees of their lower tetrachord; *nihavend*, with two intervals of an augmented 2nd; *sabah*, which differs from minoré by having a lowered 4th degree; *sega, husseini, kiourdi*, and *ousak*, with its lowered 2nd degree, which is associated with particularly sad songs in the rembetika — as an old bouzouki player said to me, 'ousak wails'. As Risto Pennanen (1997) and other scholars have pointed out, the way these modes were described and used by Greek musicians, at least by the time I and other scholars began questioning them, was somewhat different from how classically-trained Turkish musicians would have described them.

In the early rembetika, the tuning of the bouzouki and the baglama was altered to suit certain roads and songs. By the time Markos Vamvakaris dictated his autobiography he had forgotten most of these tunings or *douzenia* — again the term is a Turkish one — and there were few players who made use of them. In the days of recorded rembetika, there may have been four or five variations of the standard tuning which is d-A-D'. Of the variations, the best known is probably *karadouzeni*, literally 'black' tuning. There is some controversy about what this tuning was. According to my informants, *anikhta* or open tuning was also used (a-E-A'), as well as piraiotiko and *aravien*.

The dance rhythms

In the cafés aman at the end of the 19th century, the dances performed were of Slav, Greek and Turkish origins. The allegro, for example, was a Slav style dance in 2/4 metre resembling the Romanian *hora*, the *kasaska*, also in 2/4 metre, resembled Cossack dancing. There was also the 4/4 tsifteteli, and two dances in 9/8 metre, the zebekiko and the *aidiniko*, the first a solo male dance, the second a fast dance performed by couples.

Two of the café aman dances, the zebekiko and the tsifteteli, and a third dance which was common in Greek communities in Turkey as well as Greece, the hasapiko or butchers' dance, became the principal dances associated with the rembetika.

The commonest rhythm, and therefore the commonest dance, is the 9/4 or 9/8 zebekiko. The nine beats are broken up in several ways. In early recordings of the rembetika — most of Markos Vamvakaris's records, for example — the grouping is usually as follows:

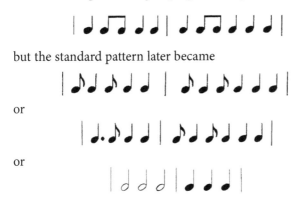

but the standard pattern later became

or

or

The hasapiko, in simple 2/4 metre, is usually broken up into eight-bar phrases coinciding with figures or patterns of dance steps. The tsifteteli has a 4/4 metre grouped in the familiar pattern of the Turkish 'belly dance', i.e.

Among the less common dance rhythms found in the rembetika are the *karsilamas*, a rapid dance in 9/8 metre; the so-called Serbian hasapiko or hasaposerviko, in 4/4 metre; and the rural folk dances like *kalamatianos* in 7/8, and *ballos* in 4/4.

The instruments

When rembetika songs were first being sung, there was a variety of instruments available in the towns which could have been used to accompany them. There were, amongst others, the outi, the santouri, violin, *tsimbalo* (cymbalum), a larger version of the santouri, kanona-ki, bouzouki, baglama, guitar, laouto, mandolin, çümbüş and saz. Early recordings, particularly those in the style of the café aman, make use of various combinations of these instruments for rembetika songs, but the bouzouki and the baglama soon became established as the basic instruments of the rembetika. The baglama was especially popular as a jail instrument and an instrument to take to the teké, being much smaller than the bouzouki and easy to hide as well as to construct. The bouzouki, on the other hand, was easier to play, and had a wider range.

Both the bouzouki and the baglama, like the Turkish saz, belong to the family of long-necked lutes. The origin of the word bouzouki is not certain. It may be from Turkish *bozuk*, meaning broken, and also broken-down as in small change, but it is possible it derives from the name of a Persian instrument or from the name of a Turkish mode. There is considerable confusion about the entire nomenclature of the bouzouki-saz family of instruments in Turkey. The baglama, for example, is the name given to a fairly large saz, but in Greek it refers only to very small instruments.

In Greece the bouzouki or an instrument very similar to it was played long before rembetika music developed. In the National Historical Museum of Greece you can see a *tambouras*, owned by the hero of the War of Independence, General Makriyannis, which closely resembles early bouzoukis. By the latter half of the 19th century, a number of paintings and engravings included representations of

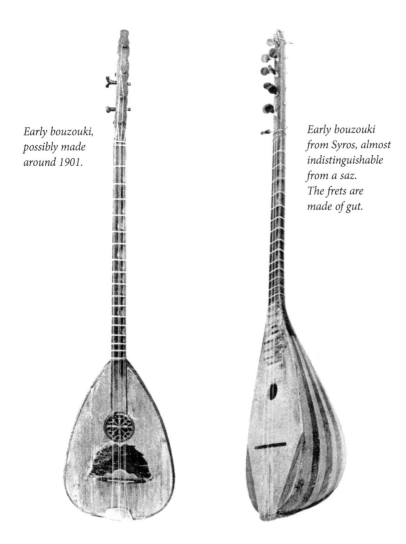

Early bouzouki, possibly made around 1901.

Early bouzouki from Syros, almost indistinguishable from a saz. The frets are made of gut.

bouzoukis. The earliest bouzouki I have seen has a repair date of 1901 and may be a good deal older. These early bouzoukis were simple instruments with gut or brass wire frets, wooden tuning pegs and frequently a sharply curving sound-box more like the modern saz. They were lightly strung and sometimes played simply with the fingernails.

The popularity of the modern bouzouki may be largely due to

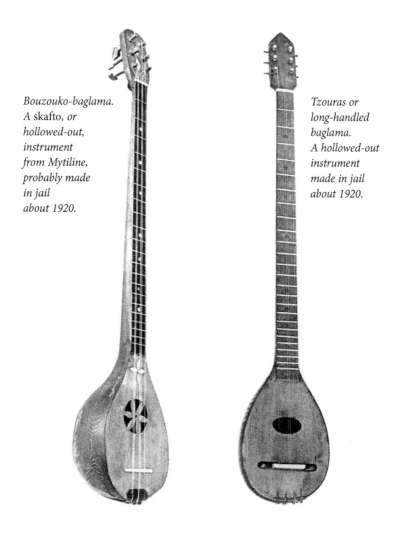

Bouzouko-baglama.
A skafto, *or*
hollowed-out,
instrument
from Mytiline,
probably made
in jail
about 1920.

Tzouras or
long-handled
baglama.
A hollowed-out
instrument
made in jail
about 1920.

the solos recorded by Ioannis ('Jack') Halikias in New York City in 1932. His version of 'To Mysterio' and 'Minore tou Deke' (sic), with the guitarist Sophocles Mikelides, enjoyed huge popularity in Greece, and was re-recorded by Spyros Peristeris and Kostas Skarvelis in Athens in the same year, although the instruments used were not, in fact, bouzoukis.

Percussion instruments were not generally used in the rembetika ensembles and a guitar was often used to supply the rhythm, but in the tekédhes and simple cafés where a player might take his baglama, the rhythm was banged out with a foot, a *komboloi* or string of worry-beads was tapped against a glass, someone might click his

Canoni or canonaki, a zither-like instrument related to the santouri, but plucked instead of struck. This inlaid instrument was made in Constantinople probably between 1900 and 1915.

fingers or clap, or spoons might be used to keep time. In establishments where women danced 'alla Turca', they usually used a tambourine or *defi* to emphasize the rhythm of the tsifteteli. Sometimes the hand-drum or *toumbeleki* was used in the café aman ensembles and female dancers often used finger cymbals.

By the 1950s the accordion and piano accordion became popular in rembetika ensembles, and the piano was also not uncommon. Tsitsanis, for example, used a woman pianist in his ensemble for many years.

The verse style

Most of the rembetika songs are written in one of the metres of Greek verse popular since the Byzantine period: iambic or trochaic metre in a line of fifteen syllables divided into two half-lines or hemistichs. However, musical accents may interrupt the normal pattern of stresses, and syllables are often stretched out or slurred over until they almost disappear. An interesting feature of the rembetika, which occurs in other Greek folk music, is the use of *tsakismata*, or exclamatory words and phrases which are metrically extraneous but are inserted into the songs from time to time. The commonest tsakisma is 'aman' or 'ach aman', but 'my mother' is also popular. Such interpolations are sometimes used to lengthen the poetic line so that it fits with the melodic line, but they often seem to have a purely emotional function. It is also common to hear musicians and singers congratulating one another on their solos or calling out to one another.

Teaching the rembetika

One of the most interesting features of the revival of the rembetika in recent years is that the Musical Conservatories of Athens and other Greek urban centres have responded to the interest by offering classes in the rembetika with the instruments used by early performers. Instruments that had all but disappeared from Greece, like the kanonaki and the outi, are now taught in Greek music schools, and many young people are learning to play them.

The nationalism that once caused some Greeks to reject the Asia Minor origins of the rembetika has faded and many younger musicians are conversant with Turkish musical traditions. International scholarship and co-operation between musicians has led to a revival of older-style rembetika, as well as a revival of music from the western part of Turkey and from Istanbul that influenced the rembetika. In towns like Mytilini, instruments that were popular there a hundred years ago are now being studied and played by the young. Rembetika music is now very popular in Turkey too, with ensembles performing it and record companies producing CDs. In a strange way, the music has made a full circle, moving from Asia Minor to Greece and back.

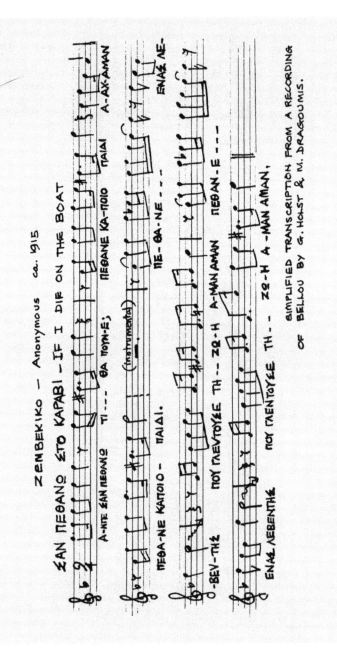

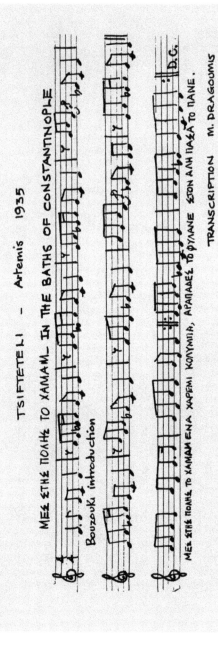

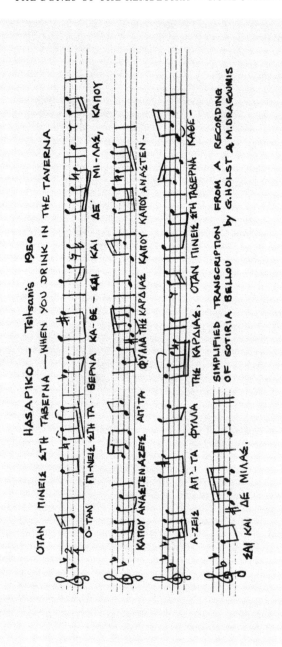

87

ΚΟΛΟΥΜΠΙ. ΦΟΡΗΤΑ
ΤΥΠΟΥ 112

Καθαρὸν βάρος τοῦ μηχανήματος 7¹/₂ χιλίγρ.

Μεγάλη ἐπιτυχία διὰ τῆς κατασκευῆς μηχανήματος-κιβωτίου. Αἱ μόναι ὑπάρχουσαι πλάκες γραμμοφώνων αἵτινες δὲν παράγουν οὐδὲ τὸν παραμικρὸν δευτερεύοντα θόρυβον.

Ἡ ὡς ἄνω εἰκὼν δεικνύει τὸ ὑλικὸν ἐκ τοῦ ὁποίου εἶναι κατεσκευασμένοι οἱ δίσκοι γραμμοφώνου «ΚΟΛΟΥΜΠΙΑ», εἰσαγόμενοι ἐξ Ἀγγλίας. Οἱ δίσκοι κατασκευάζονται συμφώνως ἐφευρέσεως, νεωστὶ βραβευθείσης.

Παριστᾶ:

Αον. Τὸ δεκτικὸν ἐξωτερικὸν ἐπίστρωμα τοῦ δίσκου, ὅπερ ἢ ἀπηλλαγμένον παντὸς δευτερεύοντος θορύβου.

Βον. Παριστᾶ τὸ ἐσωτερικὸν ὑλικὸν τοῦ δίσκου, ὅπερ εἶναι τοιαύτης δυνάμεως ὥστε οἱ δίσκοι «ΚΟΛΟΥΜΠΙΑ» (ἀγγλικὴ εἰσαγωγὴ) εἶναι οἱ ἔχοντες τὴν μεγαλυτέραν ἀντοχὴν ἐξ ὅλων τῶν τοιούτων κατασκευαζομένων.

Early Greek advertisement for a Columbia record-player.

7

Rear view, and three mileposts
on a private road

That the revival of interest in the rembetika coincided
with the 1967–74 dictatorship in Greece seems to me no accident,
although I don't think the rembetika can be described as music of
protest. It is too individualistic and disorganized for that. What I do
believe is that the rembetika has a rare power to communicate, a quality which speaks to those who feel themselves to be in some sense out-
siders. The rembetes were the drop-outs, the non-conformists of their
day. They may not have opposed social or political institutions as such,
but they made it clear that they stood outside them. They could be
jailed, beaten, chased out of town, but they would continue to live the
mangas life, speak the mangas language, wear the mangas clothes. And
it was this refusal to be brought into line with the mainstream of society which caused them to be feared both by the representatives of established authority and by the representatives of organized opposition.

It may be a slight exaggeration to say, as Petropoulos does, that the
rembetika were once considered as dangerous as leprosy, but it is
true that the songs were credited with a surprising power to influence
people. In the pre-war period, rembetika songs were banned,
bouzoukis and baglamas smashed by the police, even the dancing of
zebekiko was forbidden. Many musicians were forced to flee else-
where because conditions in Athens became intolerable. Ostensibly
the persecution was directed against hashish smoking, but investiga-
tions into the prosecution of hashish-smokers at the time reveal that
rembetika musicians were given harsher sentences than other offenders.
It was more probable that the attitude of mocking defiance, the mangas swagger which found expression in the lyrics of the rembetika
songs, was as irritating as crumbs in the bed to the stolid, repressive

puritanism of Metaxas and his police force. Not only were these manges out of line, God damn it, they were enjoying themselves.

Less understandable was the attitude of the Left, or more specifically, of the Communist Party, to the rembetika. In an article in the literary periodical *Arts Review*, in 1961, Tassos Vournas made a plea for the rembetika which he described as the 'popular musical equalizing force of the working-classes in urban centres.'[1] But from a strict Marxist point of view the songs were considered immoral because they took no cultural responsibility. In the same year, an interesting enquiry was held in the left-wing newspaper *Avghi*, where people of the musical and literary world were asked to state their opinions about the rembetika. Only one writer, Dhespina Mazaraki, made the obvious suggestion that the subject could hardly be discussed without reference to any of its creators, whom, she said, could easily be contacted through the Society of Musicians (letter to *Avghi* of 13 March 1961). One other writer was enthusiastic, but the majority condemned the rembetika as impure, 'musical slang', decadent, irresponsible. Vassilis Arkadinos (the pen-name of writer Vassilis Papadimitriou) went as far as to say that he had warned the Greek intelligentsia in 1949 about the 'power' of the rembetika, and excused the composer Theodorakis (then a communist) for using rembetika elements in his compositions only because they were part of his 'personal' creation (*Avghi*, 22 March 1961*)*. And in his biography Markos Vamvakaris describes being approached by a communist leader during the civil war and asked not to write songs about hashish because they were 'bad for the people'.

It seems that the leaders of the organized opposition were as rigid and intolerant of mangas society as the right-wing establishment, and for similar reasons: the manges were not susceptible to organization. Their own loose society was based on a common distrust of the rest of society, and their music was the creative expression of their independence.

An obvious parallel to rembetika music can be found in the urban blues of New Orleans, Chicago or Harlem. There is the same feeling

---

[1] Holst, *Δρόμος γιά τό Ρεμπέτικο*, pp. 164–84.

of being on the outside of society, the same private language ('signifying' or hip-talk and mangas slang are surprisingly similar in their inventiveness and their subject matter: hashish, jail, police and sex predominate in both), the same power to communicate suffering, the same combination of submission and defiance. The blues and the rembetika are both historical phenomena which have been allowed to degenerate and die, and have subsequently been dug up by the youth of the next generation and lovingly enshrined. Some of the reasons for the revival of interest may be unworthy — revivals are fashionable and profitable while they last — but I feel that the rembetika, like the blues, deserve their tardy recognition.

Looked at from a purely musical point of view, the rembetika songs are no more interesting or inventive than a lot of other Greek folk music. Some people would claim less. Looked at as poetry, the lyrics are uneven. At their best, they are as fresh, original and sophisticated as the demotic or *kleftic* (brigand) songs; at their worst they are banal. Generally they have a spontaneity about them which preserves them from dullness. The dances associated with the rembetika are limited, and even the zebekiko requires no great agility or skill on the part of the dancer. Bouzouki players of the 'classical' period of the rembetika seldom displayed extraordinary technique. And yet the music has a rare power to move and excite the listener. Such power is difficult to account for. I can only suggest that it has something to do with the unity of a man and his music. The words, the introduction, the dance are all still close to the magic of spontaneous creativity, and yet they have the surety of a tradition behind them, and a social framework where musician and listener are united by the mutual recognition of being outside and, in their own view, superior to the rest of society.

What I have said about the rembetika was based on a personal and incomplete journey into the world of the manges and their music. When I began looking for the rembetika, I found it elusive. Now it keeps appearing in surprising places, like Sydney, Stockholm, San Francisco. It also appeared on the Greek island of Aegina where I was living when I first wrote this book. I will leave you with a description of three friends, all of whom I met on Aegina over thirty years ago.

Yiannis drives the cesspit-emptying truck. He is in his fifties, tall for a Greek and lean — he used to play international football. His face looks as if it had been used as a nest by ferocious ants. When he dances now, only a few older heads turn to watch. His style is not showy enough for modern tastes, but he remembers the night when his uncle, a fisherman off the Piraeus coast, took him to hear the great Papaioannou playing in a club near the waterfront. 'I had no shoes, and my trousers were rolled up, but when he started to play, I couldn't keep still,' says Yiannis. 'I started dancing at the back of the room, near our own table, and I could see that Papaioannou was watching me. Then he stopped playing. "Hey you, kid!" he said. "Come over here and dance." But I was ashamed because I had no shoes on and I shook my head. Papaioannou had been smoking, I could see, and he was excited. "If you don't dance," he said, "I'll break this bouzouki in two." What could I do? He played a zebekiko, a real heavy zebekiko, and at first I was nervous, with everyone looking at me, but then I began dancing and I forgot about the people. When I stopped they went wild, and Papaioannou went on playing and I went on dancing all night. I tell you, when my uncle and I left that place there wasn't a thing that wasn't smashed. They broke the chairs and tables and plates and glasses, and they carried me out on their shoulders.'

Yiannis is still dancing, even if not many people are watching, and you can hear his truck coming a mile away — his cassette player is booming out the rembetika he loves, while he does the rounds of the cesspits.

Thanassis is a bouzouki and baglama player. He makes fine baglamas out of coconuts. He is also my teacher, although I prefer to think of him as my guru. He is in his mid-sixties, was born in Piraeus, knew Batis, Markos and Stratos, took up the bouzouki in his teens, frequented the best-known tekédhes; in fact, you might say his mangas credentials are impeccable. When it became difficult to earn a living in Piraeus playing the bouzouki, he emigrated to America where he stayed for 25 years, playing in Greek clubs and later making instruments in Greenwich Village. Now he has come back to Greece to spend his old age in peace, but he still plays his baglama in the evenings, dressed in

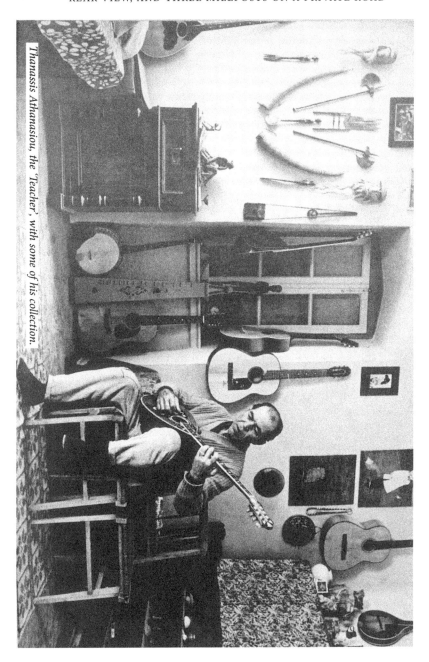

Thanassis Athanasiou, the 'Teacher', with some of his collection.

wonderfully elegant suits, with a broad-brimmed 'republican' style hat, and handmade pointed shoes that you can see your face in.

When I meet him in the morning, before he's had his coffee, he looks like a tired old man — the islanders are cheating him, prices have gone up, and Fate is writing bad things for him in the little book she keeps. But with a cup of coffee and perhaps a nip of brandy and sugar inside him, the years drop away and he takes me home to his house for a lesson. His house is a museum of musical instruments, jewellery, old watches, pictures of pretty girls in 1950s bunny costumes, his own strange paintings — one of the island, covered in trees, another of an engaging leopard crouched on a bough. Most of the things are for sale but only if you ask.

'How's Mangas?' he asks, looking fondly at the baglama he has made for me. 'He's a devil, that one, always wants to be heard, voice like a trumpet, real baritone.' He picks up his favourite baglama, which he made 25 years ago. 'This little gypsy, she's got a sweet voice — listen — that's a teké voice, not like your wild chap.' We begin to tune our instruments and he starts on a new song. 'Not that finger, the other one!' He watches me finger it wrongly again. 'No, if that finger wants to go there it must. We never force anything. Slowly, slowly. You will learn because you have a mania for it. There is plenty of time… And you must eat more — you need to be a little fatter. I know about these things.'

I look at Thanassis's match-like frame. 'But you're so thin.'

'I'm old,' says Thanassis. 'And the older you get the thinner you should be.'

Yes, Thanassi, my guru, whatever you say.

Then there is Haralambos, who lives in the village on the hill with only four houses. He heard I was interested in the rembetika, and invited me to hear him play his own songs. Haralambos is a big man in his mid-sixties. He rides by my house every morning on a small donkey. He spent most of his life working in a stone quarry and now he has his own olive press. Going into the olive press is like stepping into the middle ages. The 'factory' is so dark you can hardly see the faces of the four men unless they stand near the fire. A horse is plod-

Haralambos Maltezos and his wife Maria in the village of Pagoni, Aegina.
Maria is holding Haralambos's old bouzouki.

ding round and round turning the great crushing-stones, while the
men push a glistening tree-trunk back and forth in the press, squeez-
ing the bags of pulp. Haralambos and his son work at the press with
two other men, one of whom is a curly-haired gypsy with a single
gold earring.

Haralambos's bouzouki has been broken a dozen times and crude-
ly mended with glue. The frets are so worn that the instrument is difficult to play, but when he picks it up, there is no doubt that he is a
musician. His taximia are slow and searching, and his style of playing
is similar to the early recordings of Markos. We sit by the fire with his
fat, twinkling wife and his sombre daughter. There is no electricity,
only the flicker of the fire and the oil lamp. 'On your white arms, the
bracelets are shining,' he sings, and his wife whispers to me: 'I don't
like this music, it reminds me of when we were engaged and just look
at me now.'

For an hour he plays without stopping, one song after another, all
his own compositions. Some are hashish songs, some love songs, one
a charming sexy song about a little partridge.

Haralambos came from such a poor family that he was sent as a grocer's apprentice to Piraeus. He, too, heard Markos and Stratos, and later played in Piraeus cafés. But he came back to Aegina and worked in the quarries as his father had done. When Papaioannou came to the island to play, Haralambos was playing every week-end in a local club. Papaioannou heard him playing his own songs and said: 'What do you do for a living?'

'I work in the stone quarry,' answered Haralambos.

'You weren't born to work in a stone quarry,' said Papaioannou. 'You're as good a musician as I am, and what's more, you can sing. I never did have a voice. Come to Athens with me and you'll make a fortune.'

But Haralambos had a wife and children and a steady job, so he stayed in his village on the hill, and his rembetika stayed just as it was in the 1930s, when the tekédhes of Piraeus were flourishing.

8

Songs

The selection of rembetika song-lyrics for the first edition of this book was made partly in accordance with the availability of recordings at the time. EMIAL-Columbia (Athens) was the first record company to bring out a series of historical recordings of rembetika songs, from the private collection of Kostas Hadzidoulis, on three LPs. Entitled *Rembetiki Istoria* [*A History of Rembetika*] *1925–1955*, the series was released at the same time as *Road to Rembetika* with cover notes taken from the book. Later, the series was expanded to six LP records. In this new edition, I have substituted some of the songs and added new ones. I have also altered many of the song translations from the last edition in order to correct errors, to preserve a regular meter or to convey the spirit of a particular song in English. Since these are songs, it seems appropriate to use a regular metrical form whenever it can be done without distorting the sense. Generally I have followed the text of the first recording of the song.

ΣΑΝ ΠΕΘΑΝΩ ΣΤΟ ΚΑΡΑΒΙ

Άντε, σαν πεθάνω τι θα πούνε; Πέθανε κάποιο παιδί,
πέθανε κι ένας λεβέντης που γλεντούσε τη ζωή. Αμάν! Αμάν!

Άντε, σαν πεθάνω στο καράβι, ρίξτε με μες στο γιαλό
να με φάνε τα μαύρα τα ψάρια και το αρμυρό νερό. Αμάν! Αμάν!

ΚΟΥΒΕΝΤΕΣ ΤΗΣ ΦΥΛΑΚΗΣ

Ένα βραδάκι, βρε παιδιά, μας στήσανε καρτέρι
και μας περικυκλώσανε μέσα στου Μαουνιέρη.

Κάποιος μπαμπέσης, ο άτιμος, μαρτύρησε το χάνι
κι' ήρθαν και μας μπλοκάρανε, δώδεκα πολιτσμάνοι.

Τα γκλόπ βαρούσαν δώδεκα, κι' εμείς μαστουρωμένοι,
τρεις κάμες ξεβρακώσαμε, μα βγήκαμε χαμένοι.

Φάγαμε ξύλο, βρε άθεο, μόν' που δεν μας σκότωσαν
και όλους από τέσσερα χρονάκια μας φόρτωσαν.

ΟΜΟΛΟΓΙΕΣ

Αχ, αν δεν σου δώσει η μάνα σου ογδόντα ομολογίες,
αχ, και άλλα τόσα μετρητά, να κόψεις τις ελπίδες.

Άλλα λες και άλλα μου κάνεις,
βάλθηκες να με τρελάνεις.

Αχ, αν δεν σου δώσει η μάνα σου στην Κοκκινιά το σπίτι,
αχ, θα πάω να πάρω τη Μαριώ από τον Ποδονίφτη.

Ντούρου, ντούρου, ντούρου,
στην Πλατεία Κουμουνδούρου.

Αχ, αν δεν σου δώσει η μάνα σου σπίτι στο Περιστέρι,
αχ, και μαγαζί στον Κολωνό, δεν θα γενούμε ταίρι.

IF I DIE ON THE BOAT

Ah, if I die, what will they say? Some fellow died,
a fellow who loved life died. Aman! Aman!

Ah, if I die on the boat, throw me in the sea
so the black fish and brine can eat me. Aman! Aman!

Anonymous. George Katsaros recorded a version in the USA around 1920. This is the version Bellou recorded in the late 1960s.

CONVERSATIONS IN JAIL

One night, boys, they set us a trap
and surrounded us in Maounieris's place.

Some double-crosser fingered the joint
and a dozen cops came and raided us.

They beat us with clubs while we were all stoned;
we pulled three knives but they did us no good.

What a beating we got! It's a wonder we're here,
and all of us got four years in the pen.

Zebekiko. Ascribed to Panayiotis Toundas, early 1900s(?).

SHARES

Ah, if your mama won't give you eighty shares,
and the same in cash, forget your hopes.

You tell me one thing and you do another,
you've made up your mind to drive me crazy.

Ah, if your mama won't give you the Kokkinia house
I'll go fetch that girl Mario from Podonifti.

Dourou, dourou, doodle dourou,
in the square of Koumoudourou.

Ah, if your mama won't give you the Peristeri house
and a shop in Kolonos, we'll never make a pair.

Άλλα λες και άλλα μου κάνεις,
βάλθηκες να με πεθάνεις.

ΔΟΛΟΦΟΝΙΣΣΑ

Χωρίς καρδιά, δεν πίστευα,
χωρίς καρδιά, για να' σαι.
Σαν το κερί μ' έλιωσες,
κακούργα, μ' έκαψες,
δεν με λυπάσαι.

Γιατί με τόση απονιά
μου φαρμακώνεις την καρδιά;
Μου παίρνεις την ψυχή μου,
αχ, δολοφόνισσα κακιά.
Τα ντέρτια όλου του ντουνιά
τα δίνεις στο κορμί μου.

Κάθε φορά που θα σε ιδώ
θέλω να σε ρωτήσω,
δεν θα μ' αφήσεις μια στιγμή, κακούργα,
δίχως καημό να ζήσω;

Μα συ, κακούργα, δεν μπορείς
κακά φαρμάκια θε να βρεις,
και με να φαρμακώσεις;
Αχ, δολοφόνισσα κακια,
με δόλο και με απονιά,
στο Χάρο να με δώσεις.

ΚΑΛΟΓΕΡΑΚΙ

Καλογεράκι θα γίνω και ράσο θα φορέσω,
και κομπολόι θα κρατώ, φως μου, για να σ' αρέσω.

You tell me one thing and you do another,
the way you're going, you'll finish me off.

Syrtos. Anonymous. This version of the song also known as 'Dourou, Dourou' was recorded by Pol (Leopoldo Gad) around 1926, and another by Marika Papagika in 1928.

MURDERESS

Heartless! I didn't believe
that you could have no heart.
You melted me like a candle,
bitch, you burned me up
and you don't pity me.

Why did you poison my heart
with so much cruelty?
You take away my soul
you wicked murderess.
The pain of all the world
you heap on my poor body.

Every time I see you
I want to ask you
if you'll leave me a moment's relief
from sorrow, heartless wretch.

But you, evil woman,
want to find a poison
to poison me with.
Ah, evil murderess! With tricks
and with your heartless ways
you'll hand me over to Death.

Zebekiko. Panayiotis Toundas/Vermisoglou. Recorded by Nouros (Kostas Marselos), 1929(?).

LITTLE MONK

I'll become a little monk and wear a monkish habit,
and carry a string of worry beads, sweetheart, just to make you happy.

101

Άλλα μου λεν, άλλα μου λεν τα χείλη σου.
αλλα μου λεν τα χείλη σου και άλλα μου λεν οι φίλοι σου.
Κάλλιο έχω, βρε Βαγγελίστρα, κάλλιο έχω δυο μαχαιριές.
Κάλλιο έχω δυο μαχαιριές παρά τα λόγια που μου λες.

Καλογεράκι φτιάχτηκα, σε μοναστήρι τάχτηκα,
στα χέρια σου, γκρινιάρα μου, στα χέρια σου μπερδεύτηκα
και ξεκαλογερέυτηκα.

ΚΟΥΚΛΑΚΙ

Φίλα με στο στόμα — δε βαστώ —
δος μου ένα φιλάκι πεταχτό.
Σε αγάπησα, μικράκι μου, πολύ, κουκλάκι μου,
χάθηκα στο λάγνο σου φιλί.
Σε αγάπησα, μικράκι μου, πολύ, κουκλάκι μου,
φως μου, δεν μ' άφησες πνοή.

Τι κακό, τι απονιά,
που 'χεις για μένα, φως μου, μέσα στη καρδιά.
Στο σεβντά σου μ' έριξες, για σε πονώ, κουκλάκι μου,
ντέρτι μου 'βαλες παντοτινό.

Αχ! Αυτή η θολή σου η ματιά
μ'άναψε, μικράκι μου, φωτιά.
Μου φαρμάκωσες τη δόλια μου ζωή, κουκλάκι μου,
φως μου, δεν μου άφησες πνοή.

ΣΑΝ ΠΕΘΑΝΩ

Μάνα μου, το στήθος μου πονεί κι' αναστενάζω.
Τούτονε τον χρόνο, μάνα μου, δεν τόνε βγάζω.

Σαν πεθάνω, βρε μανούλα, μίλα στη γειτονοπούλα.
Πες της πως γι' αυτήν πεθαίνω και στον Άδη κατεβαίνω.

Your lips are saying one thing, your lips are saying one,
your lips are saying one thing, your friends say another.

I'd rather be stabbed twice, Vangelistra, rather be stabbed twice.
I'd rather be stabbed twice than hear the words you're telling me.

I got myself up as a monk and stayed in a monastery,
but I got mixed up in your hands, you nagger,
and found myself defrocked.

Zebekiko. Recorded by Zacharias Kasimatis in 1929 and ascribed to him, although there appear to be earlier versions including one recorded in the USA by K. Doussas.

LITTLE DOLL

Kiss me on the lips — I can't hold out!
Won't you blow me a kiss, little doll?
I loved you a lot, my little one, my doll,
your sexy kiss was enough to wipe me out.
I loved you a lot, my little one, my doll,
darling, you knocked the wind out of me.

What evil, what heartless cruelty,
you had in your heart for me!
You've caused me such pain, little doll,
I'm in torment because of you.

That veiled look of yours, ah!
it sets me on fire, little one.
You poisoned my wretched life, little doll,
darling, you knocked the wind out of me.

Zebekiko. Toundas. Recorded by Vangelis Sofroniou, ca. 1930.

WHEN I DIE

Mother, my chest is hurting and I sigh.
This year, mother, I won't see it out.

When I die, mother, speak to the girl next door.
Tell her I'm dying for her and I'm on my way to Hades.

Να με πλύνει, να μ' αλλάξει, το κεράκι μου ν' ανάψει,
να με πλύνει, να με κλάψει, το κορμάκι μου να θάψει.

Μάνα μου, τόπαν οι γιατροί πως έχω φθίσει,
δεν μπορεί, μανούλα μου, ο βήχας να μ' αφήσει.

ΤΑ ΧΑΝΟΥΜΑΚΙΑ

Στης Παναγιάς την αμμουδιά είχε το τεκεδάκι,
κι' ερχόμουνα κάθε πρωί κι έσπαγα νταλκαδάκι.
Δυο χανουμάκια έμορφα, μαστούρια, τα καημένα,
ένα πρωί τα τράκαρα στην άμμο καθισμένα.

Πλησίασε, ντερβίση μου, και κάθισε κοντά μου,
και άκου τραγούδια του σεβντά βγαλμένα από την καρδιά μου.
Παρ' το μπαγλαμαδάκι σου μαζί μας να φουμάρεις,
αναψ' το τσιγαλίκι σου μαζί μας να φουμαρεις.

— *Να ζήσουν τα χανουμάκια!*

Γεμίστε μου το ναργιλέ να πιω να μαστουριάσω,
κι έπειτα, χανουμάκια μου, το μπαγλαμά να πιάσω.
Να σου πατήσω ναργιλέ με τούρκικο σπαγάνι
στου Μπάρμπα-Γιάννη τον τεκέ μες το Πασαλιμάνι.

Η ΠΕΘΕΡΑ

Στου Χαροκόπου τα στενά
μια μικροπαντρεμένη
εσκότωσε τον άντρα της,
βρε, η δαιμονισμένη.

Tell her to wash me, lay me out, light a candle for me;
wash me, cry for me, and lay me in my grave.

Mother, the doctors have told me that I've got T.B.,
mother, the cough will never let me be.

*Zebekiko. Mondanaris (?). One of a number of songs in the rembetika repertoire about
tuberculosis, recorded both by Dalgas and Kostas Roukounas in the early 1930s.*

THE HANOUMAKIA

Down on the beach there was a teké,
I went there each morning to lose my blues.
I saw two girls stoned out of their minds,
sitting on the sand, poor little souls.

Come close, my dervish, and sit near me,
and hear sad songs, drawn from my heart.
Entertain us a while with your baglama,
light up a joint and smoke with us.

— *Long live the girls!*

Fill me a pipe to smoke and get high,
and later, girls, I'll take my baglama.
We'll fill you a narghilé to enjoy
at Uncle Yiannis's teké in Pasalimani.

*Zebekiko. Kostas Karipis. Recorded by Rita Abatzi in the 1930s. Hanoumakia is the
diminutive plural of hanoumi, or hanoumissa; the word is simply the Turkish word
for a woman but has the connotation in the rembetika slang of a girl who frequents
the manges circles, and most probably an Asia Minor refugee.*

THE MOTHER-IN-LAW

In the narrow streets of Harakopi
a girl who married young
killed her husband
in a fit of madness.

Στον ύπνο που κοιμότανε
μάνα και θυγατέρα
εβάλανε τον ανιψιό
και του 'ρίξε τη σφαίρα.

Βρε, Φούλα, δεν εσκέφτηκες;
Δεν πόνεσε η καρδιά σου,
τον άνδρα σου, τα νιάτα σου,
τα όμορφα παιδιά σου;

Βρε, Φούλα, πως εβάσταξες
και πως βαστάς ακόμα,
εσύ νάσαι στη φυλακή
κι' ο άντρας σου στο χώμα;

Και συ, κακούργα πεθερά,
τους πήρες στο λαιμό σου·
τη κόρη σου, τον ανιψιό,
τη δούλα, το γαμπρό σου.

Καημένε Αθανασόπουλε
τι σούμελε να πάθεις
από κακούργα πεθερά
τα νιάτα σου να χάσεις.

ΝΕΟ ΧΑΣΑΠΑΚΙ

Αγαπώ ένα χασαπάκι μες στην αγορά
που είναι ντέρτι και μεράκι κι' όλο λεβεντιά.
Θα το πάρω, δεν τ' αφήνω κι' ας βουήξει η γειτονιά,
γιατί είναι γεμάτο χάρες, γλύκιες κι' ομορφιά.

Αχ, αχ, Θεέ μου, δεν βαστώ!
Απ' την πολύ αγάπη πα να τρελαθώ.

While he lay asleep
mother and daughter
made the nephew
put a bullet through him.

Foula, didn't you think?
Didn't your heart suffer
for your husband, your youth
and fine children?

Foula, how did you bear it?
How do you stand it now,
you going to prison,
while your man lies in the ground?

And you, vile mother-in-law,
you brought them all to grief:
your daughter, your nephew,
the maid and your son-in-law.

Poor Athanosopoulos,
what did you have to suffer
from a wicked mother-in-law,
to lose all your youth!

Syrtos. Iakovos Mondanaris, 1931. The song is based on an actual murder case. Athanasopoulos was killed by a relative of his wife, Foula, at the instigation of both the mother-in-law and the wife. The record was so popular that it sold better than any other recording had ever done previously. This version was recorded by Dalgas (Andonis Diamantidis).

YOUNG BUTCHER

I love a little butcher in the market,
a sexy lad who's always full of life.
However much they talk I'll never leave him,
he's so handsome, sweet, and full of charm.

Ah, ah, my God, I can't hold out!
I'm going crazy I'm so much in love.

Αχ, αχ, Θεέ μου, δεν βαστώ!
απ' το σεβντά που έχω, πα να τρελαθώ.
Αμάν, αμάν, πολλές φορές με πλήγωσε!
Πολλές φορές με πλήγωσε, αμάν, αμάν!
Μα όχι πάλι τόσο,
αμάν, αμάν, μα όχι πάλι τόσο!
Κι' εγώ το ξέρω γρήγορα πως δεν θα τη γλιτώσω.

ΓΙ' ΑΥΤΟ ΦΟΥΜΑΡΩ ΚΟΚΑΪΝΗ

Που είν' εκείνα μου τα κάλλη,
που είναι η τόση μ' εμορφιά;
Στην Αθήνα δεν είχε άλλη
τέτοια λεβεντιά.

Ήμουν κούκλα ναι στ' αλήθεια,
με μεγάλη αρχοντιά.
Δε σας λέγω παραμύθια,
τρέλανα ντουνιά.

Μα μ' έμπλεξε ένας μόρτης,
αχ, ένας μάγκας πρώτης.
Μου πήρε ότι είχα και μ' αφήνει.

Μου πήρε την καρδιά μου,
τα νιάτα, τα λεφτά μου,
κι απ τον καημό μου φουμάρω κοκαΐνη.

— *Αχ, πανάθεμά σε, κοκαΐνη, που μ' έφαγες τι!*

Μ' αγαπούσαν αφεντάδες,
νέοι, γέροι και παιδιά,
κι όλοι οι πρώτοι κουβαρντάδες
μες στην αγορά.

Αχ, τι όμορφο περνούσα
με τραγούδια και κρασί!

Ah, ah, my God, I can't hold out!
I'm going crazy, I'm so hot for him.

Aman, aman, he's hurt me so much!
So many times, aman, aman!
But never so much, aman!
aman, aman, so much!
And I won't escape him fast.

Syrtos. Attributed to Kostas Skarvelis. First recorded by Rosa Eskenazi, 1932(?).

WHY I SMOKE COCAINE

Where have all my good looks gone,
all that beauty I had?
There wasn't another girl in Athens
who knew how to swing like me.

I was really and truly a doll,
and a classy one at that.
I'm telling you the honest truth,
I drove the whole world wild!

But I tangled with a tough guy,
a first-class mangas.
He took all I had and left me.

He took my heart,
my youth, my cash,
and from my pain I smoke cocaine.

— *Ah! a curse on you, cocaine, you've wasted me!*

The big-shots loved me,
old men and young ones,
and all the fine dudes
that hang round the market.

Ah, what fun I had
with wine and songs!

Κάθε μέρα εγλεντούσα,
τι ζωή χρυσή!

Και τώρα, η καημένη,
γυρίζω μαραμένη,
γιατί ο σεβντάς του μάγκα δε μ' αφήνει.

Με τρέλανε ο μόρτης,
ο κοκαϊνοπότης,
γι' αυτό κι εγώ φουμάρω κοκαΐνη.

ΧΑΡΙΚΛΑΚΙ

Χθες το βράδυ, Χαρικλάκι,
είχες βάλει τ' οργανάκι
και γλεντούσες μ' ένα αλάνι
κάτω στο Πασαλιμάνι.

Ζηλεύω και κλαίω,
αχ, Χαρικλάκι, πως με γέλασες!
Αμάν, μου την έσκασες!

Μες την μπύρα όταν μπήκες,
Χαρικλάκι μου, τι γλύκες,
με φωνόγραφο και πλάκες,
νταλκαδάκι με τους μάγκες.

Το πρωί για τη Γλυφάδα,
κούκλα, μ' αυτοκινητάδα.
Κολυμπάς σαν πάπια χήνα
χθες το βράδυ στην Αθήνα.

ΣΤΟΥ ΛΙΝΑΡΔΟΥ

Στου Λινάρδου την ταβέρνα
βλέπεις πρόσωπα μοντέρνα,

Every day I lived it up,
those golden days!

And now, poor me,
I wander, washed up,
hooked on my mangas still.

He drove me nuts,
the coke-head bum,
that's why I smoke cocaine too.

Tsifteteli. Toundas. Recorded by Rosa Eskenazi, ca. 1932.

HARIKLAKI

Last night, Hariklaki,
you took your instrument
and had a good time with a bum
down in Pasalimani.

I'm jealous and I cry,
ah, Hariklaki, how you made a fool of me!
Lord, what a trick you played on me!

When you came into the beer-house,
Hariklaki, what a lot of fun
with records and a phonograph
and raunchy loving with the manges.

In the morning you went to Glyfada,
doll, in a fancy car.
You went swimming like a little duck
last night in Athens.

Syrtos. Toundas, 1932. Hariklaki is the diminutive form of the girl's name Hariklia.

AT LINARDHOS'S TAVERN

At Linardhos's tavern
you see today's faces;

πάνε όλοι ένας κι' ένας
οι αστέρες της ταβέρνας·
εκεί πάει ο Παπαρούνας,
ο Βαρελλάς κι ο Μουρούνας,
πάει ο Σκόρδος ο Τεμπέλης
και ο Θρούμπας ο Τσιγκέλης.

Πάει κι' η κυρά Αγγέλω
με το μαύρο της το βέλο,
και η μερακλού η Φώτω
που μεθάει με το πρώτο.
Εκεί πάει κι' η Σταμάτα
που μεθάει και σπάει πιάτα,
πάει και η κυρά Πιπίνα
για να πιεί καμιά ρετσίνα.

Εκεί πάει ο Νταμιτζάνας,
Μαϊντανός και Μελιτζάνας,
πάει ο Ρέγγας κι' ο Μπαρδάκος,
Νεροχύτης και Δαμπάκος.
Εκεί πάει ο Χατζημπάμιας,
ο Γαρδούμπας και ο Λάμιας,
πάει κι' ο Χατζηραπάνης,
Παστουρμάς και Μπεχλιβάνης.

Σ' ένα τέτοιο ραβαΐσι
ποιος μπορεί να μη μεθύσει;
Άλλος τραγουδά, χορεύει,
κι άλλος έρωτα γυρεύει.
Άλλος πίνει και πληρώνει,
κι άλλος ζούλα την καρφώνει.
Βρε Λινάρδο, ταβερνιάρη,
γράφτο κάτω απ' το σφουγγάρι!

112

everyone goes there
the stars of the taverns:
there's Mr Poppy
and Barrel and Cod,
Lazy Garlic and
Olive the Corkscrew.

Old Mrs Angela
wears her black veil,
Foto the swinger
is drunk on one glass.
Stamata breaks plates
whenever she's drunk,
and Pepina just loves
to drink retsina.

Old Demijohn goes,
Parsley and Eggplant,
Bardakos and Herring,
Darbakos and Sink.
There's Lady's Fingers,
Gobbler and Guts,
Hadziturnip, Bully
and Bully Beef.

At such a feast
who could help getting drunk?
One dances, one sings,
and one's after love.
One drinks, one pays,
one's a sly fixer.
Write the bill, Linardhos,
where no-one will see!

*Hasapiko. Toundas. First recorded in 1932 with Dimitris Perdikopoulos singing.
Tsitsanis sang his own version of this song, substituting the name of the Thessaloniki
tavern proprietor Dalamangas for that of Linardhos.*

Ο ΩΡΩΠΟΣ

Στον Ωρωπό, καλέ, την περνάμε φίνα,
πιο καλά απ' την Αθήνα.
Τρίτη, Πέμπτη μας δίνουν μακαρόνια
κι' ο μάγκας βγάζει χρόνια.
Και την Κυριακή μας δίνουν κρέας,
τσάμπα είναι, καλέ, και ο κουρέας.

Εις το πρώτο είναι το χαρμανλίκι
και στο δεύτερο μένει το μαστουρλίκι,
και στο τρίτο το νταϊλίκι
και στο τέταρτο, καλέ, το ζοριλίκι,
και στο πέμπτο όλ' η λαθρεμπορία
και στο έκτο μένει η σκευωρία,
και στο έβδομο όλ' οι τεκετζήδες
και στο όγδοο μένουν οι ασθενήδες,
και στο νούμερο εννέα και δέκα
την αμολάνε όλοι αβέρτα.

ΣΤΗΣ ΑΘΗΝΑΣ ΤΗΣ ΟΜΟΡΦΙΕΣ

Μες της Αθήνας τις ομορφιές
ξεχωρίζει μια που καίει τις καρδιές.
Έχει μαύρα μάτια, μαύρα μαλλιά,
και στο μάγουλό της μαύρη ελιά.

Αμάν, αμάν, πα να τρελαθώ!
Από τότε που την είδα μου 'κανε κακό,
και όλο λειώνω απ' την αγάπη που 'χω στην καρδιά,
και χωρίς αυτήν δεν θα βρω γιατρειά.

Μια μέρα που την ξαναείδα, της είπα, «Κυρά μου,
έλα με με να γίνεις ταίρι για να γιάνει η καρδιά μου.»
Και μου λέει, πως αυτή, «Δεν θέλω να μ' αγαπάς,
γι' άλλονε εγώ πονώ, πάψε να με λαχταράς.»

Και από τότε ο καημένος, γέρνω πονεμένος,
και ώσπου να βγει η ψυχή μου, θε να ζω μαραδιασμένος.

OROPOS

We have a good time in Oropos jail,
better than in Athens.
Tuesday and Thursday they give us macaroni
and the manges give up years.
On Sunday they give us meat,
it's free I tell you, and so is the barber's.
In the first cell they've got the hop-heads,
in the second the chaps who are stoned;
in the third are the toughs,
in the fourth the bruisers;
in the fifth the crooked dealers go,
in the sixth the schemers,
and in the seventh the teké-owners.
The eighth is for the invalids,
and in nine and ten
they let it all hang out.

Hasapiko. Yiorgos Batis, 1933.

AMONG THE BEAUTIES OF ATHENS

Among the beauties of Athens
one stands out who sets hearts on fire.
She's got black eyes, black hair,
and a black beauty-spot on her cheek.

Lord have mercy, I'm going crazy!
From the time I first saw her she's done me no good,
and I'm wasting away from the love in my heart,
and without her I'll never be cured.

One day when I saw her, 'Lady,' I said,
'come be my girlfriend and mend my heart.'
'I don't want you to love me,' she said to me,
'I care for another, stop wanting me.'

From then on, poor me, I wander in pain,
till my soul leaves my body, I'll waste away.

Αμάν, αμάν, αμάν, γιαλελί, μεντέ ντέϊ!

ΤΟ ΠΑΡΑΠΟΝΟ ΤΟΥ ΠΡΕΖΑΚΙΑ

Απ' το καιρό που άρχισα τη πρέζα να φουμάρο
ο κόσμος μ' απαρνήθηκε, δεν ξέρω τι να κάνω.
Όπου σταθώ κ' όπου βρεθώ ο κόσμος με πειράζει
και η ψυχή μου δεν κρατά, πρέζα να με φονάζει.
Απ' τις μυτιές που τράβαγα άρχισα και βελόνι
και το κορμί μου άρχισε σιγά-σιγά να λειώνει.
Τίποτα δεν μ' απόμενε στον κόσμο για να κάνω
αφού η πρέζα μ' έκανε στους δρόμους να πεθάνω.

ΤΡΑΓΙΑΣΚΕΣ

Και οι γκόμενες φορέσανε τραγιάσκες
και στους δρόμους τριγυρνούν και κάνουν τσάρκες.
Βλέπεις γκόμενα τραγιάσκα να φοράει
και σα μαγκίτης αβέρτα περπατάει.

Και οι γκόμενες αντρίκια κουσουμάρουν
και με μάγκες τρέχουνε για να φουμάρουν.
Βλέπεις, μάγκα μου, ντερβίσικα κορίτσια
με ναζάκια, με κολπάκια και καπρίτσα.

Βλέπω μια και μια ώρα την κοιτάζω
και σα με βλέπει την τραγιάσκα κατεβάζω.
Είμαι φέρτε να της πω: «Μωρ' αδερφάκι,
ζούλα πάμε στον τεκέ για τσιμπουκάκι;»

— *Γεια σου, Μάρκο, ντερβίση μου!*

Δε μπορώ να καταλάβω, φίλοι μάγκες,
και οι κυρίες κουσουμάρουνε τραγιάσκες·

Aman, aman, aman, yieleli, mende de!

Ballos. Kostas Skarvelis. Recorded in 1933 with Rosa Eskenazi singing.

THE JUNKIE'S COMPLAINT

From the time I started to smoke the dose
the world turned its back, I'm at a loss.

Wherever I am people bother me,
I can't bear to be called a junkie.

From sniffing it up I went on the needle
and slowly my body wasted away.

Nothing was left to do in this world,
because dope led me to die in the streets.

Hasapiko. Artemis (Anestis Delias), 1934.

CAPS

And the broads put on men's caps
and they walk the streets in search of a smoke.
You see the girl who's wearing a cap
and walking like a mangas for all to see?

And the broads put on men's clothes
and off they run to smoke with the manges.
You see, mangas friend, those hip broads
with their flirting, tricks, and silly whims.

I see one and I stare at her for an hour,
and when she sees me I doff my cap.
I'm ready to tell her: 'Hey you, sister,
how about we go to the teké for a drag?'

— *Here's to you, Marko, my dervish!*

I can't understand, manges friends,
why the women are wearing caps too

— τι θα κάνουμε εμείς τα ντερβισάκια; —
μας ζυγώνουν και μας πιάνουν τα μεράκια.

Ο ΖΩΝΤΑΝΟΣ Ο ΧΩΡΙΣΜΟΣ

Για κάθε πόνο και καημό ευρέθηκε βοτάνι,
μα ο καημός του χωρισμού δεν ημπορεί να γιάνει.

Οι πίκρες και τα βάσανα με τον καιρό ξεχνιούνται,
τα μάτια όμως π' αγαπάς ποτέ δεν λησμονιούνται.

Για να ξεχάσεις κι' αν θα πάς σε ξένη μέσα χώρα
θα την θυμάσαι και θα κλαις του χωρισμού την ώρα.

Μείνε, καρδιά μου, άρρωστη με συντροφιά το κλάμα,
ν' αγαπηθείς, να χωριστείς, πες πως το 'χεις τάμα.

ΟΙ ΛΑΧΑΝΑΔΕΣ

Κάτω στα Λεμονάδικα έγινε φασαρία,
δυο λαχανάδες πιάσανε και κάναν την κυρία.

Τα σίδερα τους φόρεσαν και στη στενή τους πάνε,
κι 'αν δεν βρεθούν τα λάχανα το ξύλο που θα φάνε.

Κυρ Αστυνόμε, μη βαράς γιατί και εσύ το ξέρεις
πως η δουλειά μας είναι αυτή, και ρέφα μη γυρεύεις.

Εμείς τρώμε τα λάχανα, τσιμπούμε τις παντόφλες,
για να μας βλέπουν τακτικά της φυλακής οι όρτες.

Δε μας φοβίζει ο θάνατος, μόν' μας τρομάζει η πείνα,
γι' αυτό τσιμπούμε λάχανο και την περνούμε φίνα.

— what are we dervishes going to do? —
those broads come and steal all our fun.

Hasapiko. Markos, 1934.

PARTING GOES ON HURTING

I've found a cure for every pain and sorrow,
but the pain of separation can't be healed.

Bitterness and torment disappear;
the eyes you love can never be forgotten.

Even if you go to far-off places
you'll weep when you recall the hour you parted.

My heart, stay sick, with tears for company;
to be loved, to part, say that's what you vowed.

Hasapiko. Petropouleas. Also attributed to Skarvelis. Recorded in 1934–5 by Kavouras.

THE PICK-POCKETS

Down in Lemonadhika there was a rumpus.
They caught two pick-pockets and they acted innocent.

They put the cuffs on them and took them to the clink,
and if they don't find the loot, they'll get beaten up.

Mr Policeman, don't beat us because you know very well
this is our job, and don't expect a kick-back.

We pinch wallets and purses so the jail doors
can see us nice and regular inside.

Death doesn't scare us, it's only hunger we mind,
that's why we pick pockets and have a swell time.

Zebekiko. Evangelos Papazoglou. Recorded by Stellakis (Stelios Perpiniades) in 1934. An instant success, it was recorded almost simultaneously by several other artists.

ΤΟ ΠΑΣΟΥΜΙ

Σα σε βλέπω τα βραδάκια
στα σοκάκια να γυρνάς
και φοράς τα πασουμάκια
την καρδιά μου τη χαλάς.

Είναι κόκκινα και τρίζουν
και τη γειτονιά ξυπνούν,
όλες οι καρδιές ραγίζουν
και τις κάνουν να πονούν.

Το παπούτσι, το πασούμι,
σου ταιριάζει, βρε μικρό.
Φόρα το να ζεις και να 'σαι,
φόρα το να σε χαρώ.

Όταν βγαίνεις στην Αθήνα,
κούκλα μου, να το φοράς.
Δυο ζευγάρια κάθε μήνα
εγώ θέλω να χαλάς.

Σε κοιτάω και σε ζηλεύω,
σαν την πέρδικα πατάς.
Θα δουλεύω νύχτα μέρα
πασουμάκια να φοράς.

Η ΓΑΤΑ

Έδιωξα κι' εγώ μια γάτα
που 'χε γαλανά τα μάτια.
Σαν κοιμόμουνα τη νύχτα
μου 'χωνε βαθιά τα νύχια.

Τόσους μήνες που την είχα
μου ξηγιότανε στην τρίχα.
Τώρα έγινε από σόι
και τα ψάρια δεν τα τρώει.

THE TURKISH SLIPPER

When I see you in the evening,
walking the narrow streets,
and you're wearing Turkish slippers
you steal my heart away.

They're red and they squeak,
they wake up the neighbourhood,
and breaking every heart
make us poor men suffer.

Those shoes, those Turkish slippers,
they really suit you well.
Wear them and live it up,
wear them just to please me.

When you go out in Athens
make sure you wear them, doll.
I'd like to see you go
through two pairs every month.

I'm jealous when I look at you,
you walk just like a partridge.
Night and day I work for you
to wear those little slippers.

Ballos. Stavros Pandelides, 1934. Recorded by Rita Abatzi.

THE CAT

I threw out a cat
that had blue eyes.
When I slept at night
she dug her claws in deep.

The months I had her
she suited me fine.
Now she's taken on airs
and won't eat her fish.

Τήνε διώχνω με γινάτι
και την άλλη μέρα νάτη,
μου 'ρχεται με ποντικάκια
και μου κάνει κορδελάκια.
Τώρα βρήκα άλλη γάτα
πιο όμορφη και μαυρομάτα.
Πονηρή και αυτή σα γάτα
μου τα σπάει κρυφά τα πιάτα.

ΘΕΡΜΑΣΤΗΣ

Μηχανικός στη μηχανή και ναύτης στο τιμόνι,
κι ο θερμαστής στο στόκολο με τις φωτιές μαλώνει.

Αγάντα θερμαστάκι μου και ρίχνε τις φτυαριές σου,
μέσα στο καζανάκι σου να φτιάξουν οι φωτιές σου.

Κάργα ρασκέτα και λοστό το Μπέη να περάσω,
και μες του Κάρντιφ τα νερά εκεί να πα ν' αράξω.

Μα η φωτιά είναι φωτιά, μα η φωτιά είναι λάβρα,
και η θάλασσα μου τα 'κανε τα σωθικά μου μαύρα.

ΦΙΓΟΥΡΑΤΖΗ

Βρε, μάγκα, το μαχαίρι σου για να το κουσουμάρεις
πρέπει να 'χεις την ψυχή, φιγουρατζή, καρδιά για να το βγάλεις.

Σε μένα δεν περνάν αυτά και κρύψε το σπαθί σου,
γιατί μαστούρης θα γινώ, φιγουρατζή, και θα 'ρθω στο τσαρδί σου.

— *Για σου, Άρτεμή μου, με τις όμορφες πενιές σου!*

Αλλού να πας, φιγουρατζή, να κάνεις τη φιγούρα,
γιατί κι εγώ φουμάρισα, φιγουρατζή, κι έχω τρελή μαστούρα.

I threw her out
but she turned up next day,
bringing me mice
and trying her tricks.

Now I've found another,
more beautiful, black-eyed.
She's cunning like a cat too
and breaks plates on the sly.

Zebekiko. Stellakis / Nikos Mathesis 1934(?).

THE STOKER

Engineer at the engine, sailor at the wheel,
stoker at the stoke-hole cursing the fire.

Go to it, stoker, shovel it on,
right in the furnace, make your fires burn!

Lots of raking and poking to get through the Bay,
and in Cardiff's waters we'll drop the anchor.

But fire is fire and it throws out heat,
and the sea has turned my guts all black.

Zebekiko. Yiorgos Batis. Recorded in 1934 with the composer singing. The Bay probably refers to the notoriously rough Bay of Biscay. Cardiff: a city and port in Wales.

POSER

Hey, mangas, if you're going to carry a knife
you'd better have the guts, poser, to pull it out.

That stuff doesn't wash with me, so hide your blade
or I'll get high, poser, and come round to your shack.

— *Here's to you, Artemis, with your lovely chops!*

Go somewhere else, poser, and strut your stuff
because I've been smoking, poser, and I'm mighty high.

123

Στο 'πα να κάτσεις φρόνιμα, γιατί θα σε τσακίσω·
θα 'ρθω με το κουμπούρι μου, φιγουρατζή, και θα σε ξευτιλίσω.
— *Γεια σου ρε, Μπάτη, με το μπαγλαμά σου, μπράβο!*

ΗΡΩΙΝΗ ΚΑΙ ΜΑΥΡΑΚΙ

Να ξεφύγω δεν μπορούσα
καθώς γύριζα 'π' την Προύσα,
με προδώσαν κάτι μπράβοι
και με πιάσαν στο καράβι.

Είχα ράψει στο σακάκι
δυο σακούλες με μαυράκι
και στα κούφια μου ντακούνια
ηρωίνη ως τα μπούνια.

Θα γέμιζαν οι λουλάδες,
κλάψτε τώρα ντερβισάδες!
Θα γινότανε γιαγκίνι
με μαυράκι κι ηρωίνη.

Τώρα το 'χω βάλει τάμα,
θα μισέψω γι' άλλο πράμα.
Γεια σου, Προύσα, παινεμένη,
και στον κόσμο ξακουσμένη.

Η ΦΩΝΗ ΤΟΥ ΑΡΓΙΛΕ

— *Γεια σου, φίλε μου, Στελλάκη!*
— *Γεια και χαρά σου, Βαγγέλη μου!*
— *Τι (ει) 'ν'(αι) αυτό που κρατάς;*
— *Αργιλές!*
— *Αργιλές;*
— *Αμ, τι ήθελες να κρατώ, κανένα υπερωκεάνιο; Μα αιωνίως, μωρ' αδερφέ μου Στελλάκη, όποτ' έρθω να σε βρω, όλο με τον αργιλέ στα χέρια σε βρίσκω!*

I told you to sit tight because I'll beat you up;
I'll come with my gun, poser, and I'll call your bluff.
— *Bravo, Batis, with your baglama!*

Zebekiko. Artemis, 1935.

HEROIN AND HASHISH

I couldn't get away;
on the way back from Brusa,
two hoods fingered me
and they caught me on the boat.

I'd sewn two bags
of hashish into my jacket,
and in my hollow heels
heroin up to the top.

The pipes would have been full,
now weep, dervish lads!
There'd have been quite a party
with hashish and heroin.

Now I've made a vow
to leave it for something else.
Good-bye, famous Brusa,
known throughout the world.

Zebekiko. Sotiris Gavalas. Recorded by Stellakis, 1935.

THE VOICE OF THE NARGHILE

— *Hi there, Stellakis, my friend!*
— *Good to see you, Vangelis!*
— *What's that you're holding?*
— *A narghilé!*
— *A narghilé?*
— *Well, what did you expect me to be holding, a trans-Atlantic liner?
But it's always the same thing, brother Stellakis, whenever I come to see
you I always find you with a narghilé in your hands.*

— Αχ, φίλε μου Βάγγο, έχεις δίκαιο! Αλλά αν ήξερες και εσύ τα ντέρτια
και τα βάσανα πό 'χω, δε θα μ' αδικούσες ποτέ! Άκου, τα μωρ' αδερφέ
μου Βάγγο, να με παρηγορήσεις...

Πέντε χρόνια δικασμένος μέσα στο Γεντί Κουλέ,
από το πολύ σικλέτι το 'ριξα στον αργιλέ.

Φύσα, ρούφα, τράβα 'τόνε,
πάτα 'τόνε κι αναφτόνε.
Φύλα τσίλιες για τους βλάχους,
κείνους τους δεσμοφυλάκους.

— Πάρε κι εσύ τη δικιά σου, Βαγγέλη!
— Γεια μας!

Κι άλλα πέντε ξεχασμένος από σένανε, καλέ,
για παρηγοριά οι μάγκες μου πατούσαν αργιλέ.

— Μεγάλο το δίκιο σου, αδερφέ μου Στελλάκη!

Τώρα που 'χω ξεμπουκάρει, μες' απ' το Γεντί Κουλέ,
γέμοσε τον αργιλέ μας, να φουμάρουμε καλέ.

Φύσα, ρούφα, τράβα 'τόνε,
πάτα 'τόνε κι αναφτόνε,
φύλα τσίλιες απ' τ' αλάνι,
κι έρχονται δυο μολυσμάνοι.

— Γεια σου, ντερβίση μου Στελλάκη, που μας τα λες όμορφα!
— Γεια σου, Γιαννάκη Σεβντικιαλή, με το βιολί σου!
— Θα πιω ώσπου να πήξω σήμερα πάλι!
— Γεια σου ρε, Μαργαρώνη!

ΖΟΥΛΑ ΣΕ ΜΙΑ ΒΑΡΚΑ ΜΠΗΚΑ

Ζούλα σε μια βάρκα μπήκα
και στη σπηλιά του Δράκου βγήκα.

— You're right, my friend Vango! But if you knew the pain and troubles I have you wouldn't ever judge me wrong. Listen, brother Vango, so you can comfort me a bit....

Five years I got, in Yendi Koulé jail,
ball and chain turned me on to the narghilé.

Blow it, suck, draw it back,
turn on and light up.
Keep watch for those dummies,
the dreaded prison guards.

— Take your turn too, Vangelis!
— To our good health!

And another five years, forgotten by you,
for comfort the manges who smoked the narghilé.

— You've got one hell of a good excuse, Stellakis old buddy!

Now I'm outside, out of Yendi Koulé,
fill up our pipe and let's smoke up, my boy.

Blow it, suck, draw it back,
turn on and light up.
Keep a watch for the bum,
here come two rotten cops.

— Here's to you, you old dervish Stellakis, you tell it so nicely!
— And here's to you, Yiannaki Sevdikiali, with your violin!
— I'll keep going till I'm really stoned again today!
— Here's to you, Margaroni!

Karsilamas. Evangelos Papazoglou, 1935. Recorded by the composer with Stellakis. The two begin with a humorous dialogue, a popular device that links the songs both to the shadow puppet theatre and vaudeville traditions of the period. Yendi Koulé: the name of a prison in Thessaloniki.

SECRETLY IN A BOAT I WENT

Secretly in a boat I went
and came out at Dragon's cave.

127

Βλέπω τρεις μαστουρωμένοι
και στην άμμο ξαπλωμένοι.
Ήταν ο Μπάτης κι ο Αρτέμης
και ο Στράτος ο τεμπέλης.
Βρε συ, Στράτο, βρε συ, Στράτο,
φτιάξε ναργιλέ αφράτο.

— *Γεια σου, Στράτο, με τις ομορφιές πενιές σου!*

Να φουμάρει το Μπατάκι
που 'ναι χρόνια ντερβισάκι,
να φουμάρει κι ο Αρτέμης,
βρε, και οπου παει, βρε, και μας φέρνει.

Μας στέλνει μαύρο απ' την Πόλη
και μαστούρια είμαστε όλοι,
τουμπεκί απ' την Περσία
πίνει ο μάγκας με ησυχία.

— *Γεια σου, Αρτέμη!*

ΟΤΑΝ ΔΩ ΤΑ ΔΥΟ ΣΟΥ ΜΑΤΙΑ

Ραντεβού σαν περιμένω όταν αργήσεις βαριεστώ
κι όταν δω τα δυο σου μάτια όλα, φως μου, τα ξεχνώ.

Πείσματα να μη μου κάνεις άπονη, κακία μικρή,
γιατί μ' αυτά σου τα ναζάκια με κατάντησες μπεκρή.

Μέρα νύχτα στις ταβέρνες ξενυχτάω και μεθώ,
για τα δυο σου τα ματάκια, μόρτισσα, θα τρελαθώ.

ΟΣΟΙ ΓΙΝΟΥΝ ΠΡΩΘΥΠΟΥΡΓΟΙ
(Ο Μάρκος Υπουργός)

Όσοι γίνουν πρωθυπουργοί, όλοι τους θα πεθάνουν,
τους κυνηγάει ο λαός απ' τα καλά που κάνουν.

I saw three men stoned on hashish
stretched out on the sand.

It was Batis and Artemis
and Stratos the lazy one.
Hey you, Stratos, yes you, Stratos,
fix us a fine narghilé!

— *Here's to you, Stratos, with your lovely riffs!*

So Batis can have a smoke,
who's been a head for years,
and Artemis can smoke too,
who brings us back dope wherever he goes.

He sends us Istanbul hashish
and all of us get high,
and fine Persian tobacco
for the mangas to smoke in peace.

— *Here's to you, Artemis!*

Zebekiko. Batis. Recorded in 1935 by Stratos.

WHEN I SEE YOUR TWO EYES

When you're late for our meeting I'm sad,
but I see your two eyes, darling, and forget it.

Don't hold out on me, hard-hearted hussy,
your flirting has made me a drunkard.

Night and day I stay up in the taverns,
I'll go mad, little tramp, for those eyes.

Zebekiko. Papaioannou. Recorded in 1935 or 1936 with the composer singing.

THOSE WHO BECOME PRIME MINISTERS
(Markos the Minister)

Those who become Prime Ministers are sure to die of it;
the people hunt them down because of the good they do.

Πέθανε ο Κονδύλης μας, πάει κι' ο Βενιζέλος,
την πούλεψε κι' ο Δεμερτζής που θα 'φερνε το τέλος.
— *Γεια σου, ρε Μάρκο, με το ζοριλίκια σου!*

Βάζω υποψηφιότητα πρωθυπουργός να γίνω,
να κάθομαι τεμπέλικα να τρώω και να πίνω.
Και ν' ανεβαίνω στη βουλή, εγώ να τους διατάζω,
να τους πατώ το ναργιλέ και να τους μαστουριάζω.

ΜΕΣ ΤΗΣ ΠΟΛΗΣ ΤΟ ΧΑΜΑΜ

Μες της πόλης το χαμάμ, ένα χαρέμι κολυμπάει,
αραπάδες το φυλάνε, στον Αλή Πασά το πάνε.

Διατάζει τη φρουρά του να τις φέρουνε μπροστά του,
να τις βάλει να χορέψουν και μπουζούκια να του παίξουν.

Αργιλέδες να φουμάρει με χασίσι τούρκικο
και χανούμια να χορεύουν τσιφτετέλι γύφτικο.

Έτσι την περνάνε όλοι οι πασάδες στον ντουνιά,
μ' αργιλέδες, με μπουζούκια, μ' αγκαλιές και με φιλιά.

ΦΡΑΓΚΟΣΥΡΙΑΝΗ

Μια φούντωση, μια φλόγα, έχω μέσα στην καρδιά,
λες και μάγια μου 'χεις κάνει, Φραγκοσύριανη γλυκειά.

Θα 'ρθω να σε ανταμώσω πάλι στην ακρογιαλιά,
θα 'θελα να με χορτάσεις όλο χάδια και φιλιά.

Θα σε πάρω να γυρίσω Φοίνικα, Παρακοπί,
Γκαλισσά και Ντελαγκράτσια, και ας μου 'ρθει συγκοπή.

Στο Πατέλι, στο Νιοχώρι, φίνα στην Αληθινή,
και στο Μπισκοπό ρομάντσα, γλυκειά μου Φραγκοσυριανή.

Our Kondylis died, and Venizelos too,
Demerdzis kicked the bucket before he solved a thing.

— *Here's to you, Markos, you tough guy!*

I think I'll be a candidate for Prime Minister,
so I can laze about eating and drinking all day.

I'll stand up in the parliament and order them about,
and pass around the hookah and make sure they're all stoned.

Zebekiko. Markos. Recorded in 1936 by Markos without the second stanza.

IN THE BATHS OF CONSTANTINOPLE

In the baths of Constantinople a harem's swimming;
Arabs guard them, take them to Ali Pasha.

He orders his guards to bring them before him,
to make them dance and play the bouzouki.

So he can smoke the hookah with Turkish hashish
while the ladies dance the gypsy tsifteteli.

That's how the pashas live in this world,
with hookahs, bouzoukis, and kisses galore.

Tsifteteli. Artemis. Recorded in 1936.

FRANKOSYRIAN GIRL

There's a spark, a flame inside my heart,
you must have bewitched me, Frankosyrian girl.

I'll come to meet you again on the shore,
I'd like to gorge myself on caresses and kisses.

I'll take you to Finika, Parakopi,
Galissa and Delagratsia, even if I die.

To Pateli, Neohori and Alithini,
romance at Biskopio, sweet Frankosyriani!

Hasapiko. Markos, 1936.

ΡΙΞΕ, ΤΣΙΓΓΑΝΑ, ΤΑ ΧΑΡΤΙΑ

Ρίξε, τσιγγάνα, τα χαρτιά και πες μου την αλήθεια,
θα γειάνει τάχα ο καημός που έχω μες στα στήθεια;

Πες μου ο πόνος της καρδιάς θα γιατρευτεί λιγάκι,
η θα χαθούν τα νιάτα μου απ' το πολύ φαρμάκι;

Πες μου, τσιγγάνα, και φλουριά εγώ θα σε γεμίσω,
την κόρη που μ' απαρνήθηκε αν την ξαναποχτήσω.

ΝΤΥΜΕΝΗ ΣΑΝ ΑΡΧΟΝΤΙΣΣΑ

Σε θέλω να 'σαι μάγκισσα, με τσαχπινιά και νάζι,
κι όλος ο κόσμος τι θα πει, Μαρίτσα μου, ποτέ να μη σε νοιάζει.

Ντυμένη σαν αρχόντισσα μαζί μου να γυρίζεις,
να πίνεις σαν παλιός μπεκρής, κουκλίτσα μου, με σκέρτσο να
    καπνίζεις.

Να βάζεις τη φουστίτσα σου με γούστο και μεράκι,
και στο ποδάρι να φοράς, Μαρίτσα μου, το πιο καλό γοβάκι.

Να 'σαι τσαχπίνα κι' έξυπνη, τον κόσμο να πειράζεις,
και στην καρδιά σου καημό, Μαρίτσα μου, ποτέ σου να μη βάζεις.

ΠΕΣ ΤΟ ΝΑΙ ΚΙ ΑΣ ΕΙΝΑΙ ΨΕΜΑ

Δεν ξέρω, βρε κουκλάκι μου, γιατ' έτσι με παιδεύεις,
την θέλεις την αγάπη μου η με κοροϊδεύεις;

Πες το ναι κι ας είναι ψέμα,
μπρος γκρεμός και πίσω ρέμα!

Μικρούλα, εγώ σε γνώρισα μέσα στη γειτονιά μου
κι απ' όλες σε ξεχώρισα και σ' είχα στην καρδιά μου.

Μου 'χες πει σαν μεγαλώσεις
την καρδιά σου θα μου δώσεις.

THROW DOWN THE CARDS, GYPSY

Throw down the cards, gypsy, and tell me the truth,
will this pain in my breast ever be cured?

Will it get a little better, this pain in my heart,
or will all this poison destroy my youth?

Tell me, gypsy, and I'll load you with coins,
will I get back the girl who turned me down?

Zebekiko. Markos, ca. 1937.

DRESSED LIKE A LADY

I want you to be a mangas girl, naughty and full of fun,
and whatever people say, Maritsa, don't let it bother you.

Dressed like a lady, doll, you'll go around with me,
and you'll drink like a drunkard and smoke in style.

You'll put your skirt on in the sauciest way, Maritsa,
and the best pair of heels in town.

Be sexy and smart, turn the world on its head,
and don't let the blues get inside your heart.

Zebekiko. Stelios Keromitis. Recorded by Daisy Stavropoulou in 1937(?).

SAY YES, EVEN IF YOU LIE

I don't know why you torment me so, little doll,
do you want my love or are you only teasing?

Say yes, even if you lie,
a ravine's in front, a gorge behind!

I knew you in our neighbourhood, my sweet,
I picked you out and kept you in my heart.

You told me when you grew up
you'd give your heart to me.

Μα τώρα που μεγάλωσες κι έγινες κοπελίτσα,
γιατί τη γνώμη άλλαξες, ωραία μου κουκλίτσα;

Πες το ναι κι ας είναι ψέμα,
μπρος γκρεμός και πίσω ρέμα!

ΠΑΙΧΝΙΔΙΑΡΑ

Πίστεψέ με, παιχνιδιάρα,
πως για σένα δεν δίνω διάρα!
Το πολύ σου σκέρτσο,
το πολύ σου νάζι,
άρχισε και με πειράζει.

Στην αρχή μ' είχες τυλίξει,
έτσι θα μου τα 'χεις ρίξει,
και πολλά φαρμάκια ήπια
χίλια μου 'κανες τερτίπια.

Τώρα πια δεν σου τ' αρνιέμαι
μα άρχισα να σε βαριέμαι.
Με κουράσαν τα φιλιά σου
κι η μπαμπέσα η καρδιά σου.

Το πολύ σου σκέρτσο,
το πολύ σου νάζι,
άρχισε να με κουράζει.

ΛΙΤΑΝΕΙΑ

Σαν χριστιανός ορθόδοξος σ' αυτήν την κοινωνία,
εβάλθηκα, ρε μάγκα μου, να κάνω λιτανεία.

Ψωνίζω τις τζουρίτσες μου κι' ένα κομμάτι μαύρο,
και ξεκινώ, ρε μάγκα μου, να πάω στον Άγιο Μάμα.

But now you've grown into a fine young lady,
why have you changed your mind, pretty doll?

Say yes, even if you lie,
a ravine's in front, a gorge behind!

Zebekiko. Kostas Karipis, 1938(?). First recorded with Ioanna Yiorgakopoulou and Keromitis.

TEASER

Believe me, teaser,
I don't give a sou for you!
All your flirting,
all your smooching,
has begun to bother me.

You had me all tied up,
at first that's how you got me in.
I swallowed a lot of poison
with the thousands of tricks you played.

Now I don't deny it,
I'm getting tired of you.
I'm tired of all your kisses
and tired of your tricky heart.

All your flirting,
all your smooching,
has begun to bother me.

Tsifteteli. Keromitis, 1938.

THE LITANY

Like an Orthodox Christian in this society,
I set out, mangas, to hold a litany.

I shop for tobacco ends and a piece of hashish
and I make my way to St Mamas's.

Ανάμεσα στην εκκλησία στις στρόγγηλες καμάρες
ανάψαμε το ναργιλέ, σαν νά 'τανε λαμπάδες.
Και ο αρχάγγελος αποκεί με μια μεγάλη φούρια·
απ' τα ντουμάνια τα πολλά τον έπιασε μαστούρα.
Μου λέει, «Άκου, χριστιανέ, δεν είναι αμαρτία
που μπήκες μες στην εκκλησιά να κάνης λιτανεία.»
Μα ξάφνου κι ένας καλόγερος μου λέει, «Τράβα πίσω,
γιατί κι' εγώ έχω σειρά καμιά για να ρουφήξω.»

ΔΕΝ ΜΟΥ ΛΕΣ ΤΟ ΝΑΙ ΚΑΙ ΕΣΥ;

Το χρήμα δεν το λογαριάζω,
τα δυο σου μάτια σαν κοιτάζω·
δυο μαύρα μάτια σαν κι' αυτά
αχ! δεν τα βρίσκω με λεφτά.

Έλα να σμίξουμε, μικρό μου,
και να σε νοιώθω στο πλευρό μου.
Γω δεν σ' αλλάζω με καμιά
κι' αν μου χαρίζουν το ντουνιά.

Βλέπεις εντάξει σου ξηγιέμαι
πως σε λατρεύω δεν τ' αρνιέμαι.
Είσ' η λαχτάρα μου η χρυσή,
γιατί δε λες το ναι και συ;

ΟΜΟΡΦΗ ΜΕΛΑΧΡΙΝΗ

Μια όμορφη μελαχρινή, ναζιάρα και σκερτσόζα,
τόσο πολύ με τυραννεί, που μου κρατάει πόζα.

Θα τη ζυγώσω μια βραδιά και θα την ερωτήσω,
πως γίνεσαι τόσο κακιά; Για σένα θα αρρωστήσω!

Under the church's rounded arches
we lit the narghilé as if it was a candle.

And the archangel arrives in a rush;
he's got quite high on all the smoke.

'Listen Christian,' he says, 'it's no sin
that you came here to say the litany.'

But suddenly a monk says: 'Get back!
It's my turn to have a drag.'

Zebekiko. Tsitanis, 1938. Not recorded, for obvious reasons, until 1983.

WHY NOT SAY YES TOO?

I don't think of money
when I see your eyes;
two eyes like those,
ah! I can never buy.

Let's get together
so I feel you beside me.
I wouldn't exchange you
for all the world.

See, I tell you it straight,
I adore you.
My golden desire,
why not say yes too?

Hasapiko. Kostas Karipis, ca. 1938. Recorded by Ioanna Yiorgakopoulou and Kero-mitis.

BEAUTIFUL BRUNETTE

A beautiful brunette, a teaser, a flirt,
she treats me so badly, puts on such airs.

I'll go up and ask her one night, I'll say:
how come you're so bad? You're making me ill!

Τα κατσαρά σου τα μαλλιά, τα μάτια σου τα μαύρα,
μες τη δική μου αγκαλιά θα σβήσουν κάθε λαύρα.

ΜΕΣ ΤΗΣ ΠΕΝΤΕΛΗΣ ΤΑ ΒΟΥΝΑ

Με στης Πεντέλης τα βουνά, μανούλα μου, στα πεύκα τριγυρίζω,
τον Χάρο ψάχνω για να βρω, μα δεν τόνε γνωρίζω.

Ένα γλυκό ξημέρωμα το Χάρο ανταμώνω,
μες της Πεντέλης τα βουνά, μανούλα μου, και του μιλώ με πόνο:

«Χάρο», του λέω, «άσε με ακόμα για να ζήσω·
έχω γυναίκα και παιδιά, μανούλα μου, πες μου που θα τα' αφήσω;»

Με βλέπει και χαμογελάει κι' αρχίζω πια να σφίνω,
μου λέει με δυνατή φωνή, μανούλα μου, «Σε παίρνω, δεν σ' αφήνω.»

ΝΑΖΙΑΡΑ

Ναζιάρα μ' έχεις μπλέξει
μ' αυτή την πονηριά,
κι έξυπνα μου 'χεις κλέψει,
μικρή μου, την καρδιά.

Τυλίχτηκα σαν ψάρι
στο δίχτυ σου, κουκλί,
και μου 'χεις πια για πάντα
σκλαβώσει τη ζωή.

Ναζιάρα μου, τσαχπίνα,
κουκλίτσα μου χρυσή,
η μόνη μου λαχτάρα
κι' ο κόσμος είσαι εσύ.

Your curly hair and your two black eyes
will quench every fire when you're in my arms.

Hasapiko. Markos, 1938–9.

IN THE MOUNTAINS OF PENDELI

In the mountains of Pendeli, oh mother, I walk among the pines,
and look for Death although he is a stranger.

In the mountains of Pendeli, oh mother, one sweet break of day,
we meet at last and painfully I speak:

'Leave me Death, some time to live ⊠ I have a wife,' I say,
'and children too, oh mother, and don't know how to leave them.'

He sees me and smiles, oh mother, and I start to fade away;
in a loud voice he says: 'I take you, I don't leave you.'

Zebekiko. Stratis, 1939.

FLIRT

You've got me tied up
with your cunning ways,
you've cleverly stolen
my heart, little one.

I'm caught like a fish
in your net, my doll,
you've made me your slave
for my whole life.

My sexy flirt,
my golden doll,
my one desire,
and my whole world.

Hasapiko. Dimitris Perdikopoulos. Recorded by Keromitis in 1939.

ΔΙΧΩΣ ΚΑΡΑΒΟΚΥΡΗ

Είμαι μικρούλα κι' ορφανή
από μάνα κι από κύρη,
σαν τη βαρκούλα στο γιαλό
δίχως καραβοκύρη.

Με δέρνουν όλοι οι καιροί
και με χτυπάει το κύμα,
έτσι να βασανίζομαι,
Χριστέ, δεν είναι κρίμα!

Γύρισε, ρίξε μια ματιά,
κοίτα την κατάντια μου,
Χριστέ μου συ, λυπήσου με,
και Παναγιά κυρά μου.

Καλόγρια, θε, να γίνω,
να σώσω την ψυχή μου,
για να μη βασανίζεται
το δόλιο το κορμί μου.

ΣΑΛΤΑΔΟΡΟΣ

Ζηλεύουνε, δεν θέλουνε ντυμένο να με δουν,
μπατίρη θέλουν να με δουν για να φχαριστιθούν.

Θα σαλτάρω, θα σαλτάρω,
τη ρεζέρβα να τους πάρω.

Μα γω πάντα βολεύομαι γιατί τηνε σαλτάρω
σε καν' αμάξι γερμανό και πάντα τη ρεφάρω.

Σάλτα, σάλτα, θα σαλτάρω,
τη ρεζέρβα να σου φάω.

Βενζίνες και πετρέλαια εμείς τα κυνηγούμε
γιατ' έχουνε πολλά λεφτά και φίνα την περνούμε.

WITHOUT A HELMSMAN

I'm young and an orphan
without a mother or father,
like a boat at sea
without a helmsman.

All weathers buffet me
and the waves hit me;
Christ, isn't it a shame
to be tormented like this!

Spare a glance for me,
look at the state I'm in;
Christ take pity on me
and my Lady, the Virgin.

I'll become a nun
to save my soul,
so that my wretched body
won't suffer any more.

Hasapiko. Memetis. First recorded in 1939 with Ioanna Yiorgakopoulou singing.

THE JUMPER

They're jealous, they don't want to see me dressed up,
they'll only be happy when they see me broke.

I'll jump, I'll jump,
I'll take their jerry-cans.

But I always manage because I jump
on a German truck, and I always share it.

I'll jump, I'll jump,
I'll swipe your jerry-can.

It's petrol and kerosene we're after;
they're worth a fortune and we live it up.

Σαν πουλήσω τη ρεζέρβα
θα την πιω να γίνω τέζα.

Κι' όταν ρίξω και καμιά, ρεζέρβα που την λένε,
την πάω για τον νταβατζή κι' αμέσως κονομιέμαι.

Σαν αρπάξω τη ρεζέρβα
είναι ντου και σήκω φεύγα.

Η ΔΡΟΣΟΥΛΑ

Άνω κάτω χθες τα κάνανε
στου Σιδέρη τον παλιό τεκέ.
Πρωί πρωί με τη δροσουλα
επάνω στη γλυκιά μαστούρα.
Στήσανε καυγά δυο μάγκες
για να κάνουν ματσαράγκες.

Τεκετζή μου βάστα να σου πω,
σου μιλάει ο μάγκας με καημό.
Το χασίσι κι αν φουμάρω
εγώ κανένα δεν πειράζω.
Είμαι μάγκας και αλάνης
κι' ήρθα στον τεκέ χαρμάνης.

Μπήκα μόνος μέσα στον τεκέ
να φουμάρω ένα ναργιλέ,
να φουμάρω να μπαφιάσω,
και τις πίκρες να ξεχάσω.
Μες την τόση μου σκοτούρα
βρίσκω ωραία στη μαστούρα.

142

When I sell that jerry-can
I'll drink until I'm stewed.

And when I throw a 'spare' from the truck
I'm off to the dealer and it's cash on the line.

When I snatch that jerry-can
it's off with me, I hit the road.

Zebekiko. Written by Mihailis Yenitsaris during the German occupation (1942?) but not recorded at the time.

THE DEW

They turned Sidheris's teké
upside down yesterday.
Early in the morning it was,
with the dew still on the grass.
Two manges started a fight
to do their dirty work.

Listen, I tell the owner,
the mangas speaks to you
with sadness. If I smoke
hashish, I bother no-one.
I'm a mangas and a bum and I came
to the teké because I needed a smoke.

I came to the teké alone
to smoke a narghilé,
to smoke, get really high,
and drive my bitterness away.
In my black despair
I feel fine when I'm stoned.

Zebekiko. Tsitsanis, 1944. First recorded in 1945(?) with Tsitsanis and Markos. Miltos Sidheris had a teké on Nikiforos Fokas Street in Thessaloniki.

ΧΡΟΝΙΑ ΜΕΣ ΤΗΝ ΤΡΟΥΜΠΑ

Χρόνια μες την Τρούμπα,
μαγκίτης κι' αλανιάρης,
φρόντισε να μάθεις
κι ύστερα να με πάρεις.

Είμαι παιδάκι έξυπνο,
παίζω και μπουζουκάκι·
όλος ο κόσμος μ' αγαπάει
γιατί είμαι Συριανάκι.

Στην πιάτσα που μεγάλωσα
όλοι μ' έχουν θαυμάσει
γιατί είμαι μάγκας κι' έξυπνος
και σ' όλα μου εντάξει.

Οι μάγκες με προσέχουνε
κι' όλοι με λογαριάζουν.
Όταν με βλέπουν κι' έρχομαι
μαζί μου νταλκαδιάζουν.

Ο ΚΑΛΟΓΕΡΟΣ

Βαρέθηκα τις γκόμενες,
κοντεύω να τα χάσω,
γι' αυτό και τ' αποφάσισα
να σε φορέσω ράσο.

Όσα λεφτά οικονόμησα
φράγκο δεν αποχτούσα.
Μαζί μ' αυτές τα χάλασα
και ρέστος τριγυρνούσα.

Μπελάδες και τραβήγματα,
ξενύχτια φασαρίες,
και ταχτικά τραβιόμουνα
και πλήρωνα αμαρτίες.

YEARS IN TROUMBA

Years in Troumba,
mangas and street-boy,
make sure you check it out
before you take me on.

I'm a clever lad
and I play the bouzouki;
everyone loves me
because I'm from Syros.

In the place I grew up
they all admire me
'cos I'm a smart mangas
whatever I do.

The manges all
take notice of me.
When they see me coming
they're on my side.

Zebekiko. Markos, 1945.

THE MONK

I'm tired of women,
I'm about to lose my mind.
That's why I've decided
to put a monk's robe on,

Whatever cash I've saved
I never kept a cent.
I spent it all on them
and gone around like a pauper.

All that trouble and strife
and nights spent quarrelling,
the pain goes on and on
and I've paid for all my sins.

Τώρα θ' αλλάξω πια ζωή,
δε θα με λεν μπατίρη,
και πάω για καλόγερος
σε κάποιο μοναστήρι.

ΤΟ ΚΑΠΗΛΕΙΟ

Η νύχτα είναι παγερή και σιγοψιχαλίζει,
κι' απ' την απέναντι γωνιά το καπηλειό φωτίζει.

Κι' ένας απένταρος μπεκρής, έξω απ' το ταβερνάκι,
συλλογισμένος κάθεται στο χαμηλό πορτάκι.

Θέλει να μπει κι' αυτός εκεί ν' αρχίσει και να πίνει,
μα είναι φτωχό το καπηλειό και βερεσέ δεν δίνει.

ΠΟΣΕΣ ΚΑΡΔΟΥΛΕΣ ΚΛΑΨΑΝΕ

Πόσες καρδούλες κλάψανε σ' αυτά τα μαύρα χρόνια
που ζήσαμε μες στη σκλαβιά και μες στην καταφρόνια;

Πόσα κορμάκια πήγανε και νιάτα έχουν σβήσει,
και πόσα σπίτια από άδικο για πάντα έχουν κλείσει;

Η μαύρη με το Γερμανό έγιναν η αιτία
που το λαό μας ρίξανε σε τόση δυστυχία.

Ας όψονται οι αίτιοι που κάψαν την καρδιά μας
και πλούτησαν και γλέντησαν με την απελπισιά μας.

ΚΑΠΕΤΑΝ ΑΝΔΡΕΑΣ ΖΕΠΟΣ

Μια ψαροπούλα είναι αραγμένη
στο ακρογιάλι το Ζέπο περιμένει.
Καπετάν Ανδρέα Ζέπο
χαίρομαι όταν σε βλέπω.

146

Now I'll change my life,
no-one will say I'm broke.
I'll go and be a monk
in some monastery or other.

Hasapiko. Markos, 1945.

THE LITTLE WINE-SHOP

The night is chilly and a soft rain falls;
on the opposite corner, the wine-shop's lit up.

Outside the little shop a penniless drunk
sits thoughtfully in the low doorway.

He'd like to go in too and drink
but the wine-shop's poor and they give no credit.

*Zebekiko. Batis. Recorded in the mid 1940s with Ioanna Yiorgakopoulou and the
composer singing.*

HOW MANY HEARTS WEPT

How many hearts wept in those black years
that we lived in slavery, treated like dirt?

How many young bodies and lives were wiped out?
How many homes shut forever for this crime?

The German black market caused it all;
it forced our people into misery.

Let them see, those who made our hearts burn,
and got rich and enjoyed themselves on our despair.

Zebekiko. Stratos, 1946.

CAPTAIN ANDREAS ZEPOS

A fishing-boat is tied up
waiting on the shore for Zepos.
Captain Andreas Zepos
I'm happy when I see you.

Όλοι καλάρουνε μα δεν βγάζουν ψάρια,
καλάρει ο Ζέπος και βγάζει καλαμάρια.
Έγια μόλα! Έγια λέσα!
Έχει ο σάκος ψάρια μέσα;

Όλοι στο τσούρμο μας είμαστε ιππότες,
εφτά απ' την Κούλουρη και τρεις Αϊβαλιώτες.
Έγια μόλα! Έγια λέσα!
Έχει ο σάκος ψάρια μέσα;

ΤΡΕΞΕ ΜΑΓΚΑ ΝΑ ΡΩΤΗΣΕΙΣ (Η Ντερμπεντέρισσα)

Τρέξε, μάγκα, να ρωτήσεις, να σου πουν, πια είμ' εγώ.
Είμ' εγώ γυναίκα φίνα, ντερμπεντέρισσα,
που τους άντρες σαν τα ζάρια τους μπεγλέρισα.

Δε με συγκινούν αγάπες, φτάνει να καλοπερνώ.
Κάθε βράδυ να τραβάω το ποτήρι μου
και να σφάζονται λεβέντες για χατίρι μου.

Πως θα γίνω εγώ δική σου, πάψε να το συζητάς.
Δε γουστάρω τις παρόλες, σου ξηγήθηκα,
στις ταβέρνες και στα καμπαρέ γεννήθηκα!

ΨΑΡΟΠΟΥΛΑ

Ξεκινάει μια ψαροπούλα, απ' το γιαλό,
ξεκινάει μια ψαροπούλα, απ' την Ύδρα τη μικρούλα,
και πηγαίνει για σφουγγάρια, όλο γιαλό.

Έχει μέσα παλικάρια, απ' το γιαλό,
έχει μέσα παλικάρια που βουτάνε για σφουγγάρια,
γιούσερ κι' όμορφα κοράλια, απ' το γιαλό.

Έχει Συριανούς, Καλύμνιους, απ' το γιαλό,
έχει Υδραίους και Ποριώτες, Αιγινήτες και Σπετσιώτες
που βουτάνε για σφουγγάρια, από γιαλό.

They all cast their nets and come up with no fish,
Zepos casts his and pulls up fine squid.
Heave-ho! Heave-ho!
Are there any fish in the bag?

We're all fine gents in our crowd,
Seven from Koulouri and three from Aivali.
Heave-ho! Heave-ho!
Are there any fish in the bag?

Syrtos. Papaioannou. First recorded in 1946–7.

RUN AND ASK THEM, MANGAS (A Swinging Dame)

Run and ask them, mangas, to tell you who I am.
I'm a great woman, a real swinger,
and I've played men, like dice, through my fingers.

Love doesn't move me, a good time's enough.
Every evening I keep on drinking
while brave lads kill each other for me.

Stop asking me how I can be all yours.
I don't care for words, I made it clear,
I was born in the taverns and cabarets.

Zebekiko. Tsitsanis. Recorded in 1947 with the composer and Stella Haskil singing.

FISHING-BOAT

A fishing-boat sets out from the shore,
a fishing-boat sets out from little Hydra,
it's going after sponges, all along the shore.

And brave lads are on board, from the shore,
brave lads are on board who dive for sponges,
black and pretty coral, from the shore.

They're from Symi and Kalymnos, from the shore,
Hydra, Poros, Aegina and Spetsas,
who all dive for sponges, from the shore.

Γεια χαρά σας παλικάρια, και στο καλό,
γεια χαρά σας παλικάρια, να μας φέρετε σφουγγάρια,
γιούσερ και μαργαριτάρια, απ' το γιαλό.

ΟΤΑΝ ΠΙΝΕΙΣ ΣΤΗΝ ΤΑΒΕΡΝΑ

Όταν πίνεις στην ταβέρνα, κάθεσαι και δεν μιλάς,
κάπου κάπου αναστενάζεις απ' τα φύλλα της καρδιάς.
Θα 'θελα να σε ρωτήσω και να πληροφορηθώ
ποιο μεράκι σ' έχει κάνει τόσο μελαγχολικό;
Μήπως έχεις αγαπήσει και προδόθηκες και συ.
Έλα, κάθισε κοντά μας, να γλεντήσουμε μαζί.

ΣΑΤΡΑΠΙΣΣΑ (Αραμπάς περνά)

Αραμπάς περνά, αραμπάς περνά,
κι' η σατράπισσα που αγάπησα είναι μέσα.
Αγκαλιάζεται κι' ούτε νοιάζεται, η μπαμπέσα.

Αραμπάς περνά, αραμπάς περνά,
με τη βλάμισσα που χαράμησα τη ζωή μου.
Με ρεστάρησε, στραπατσάρησε το τσαρδί μου.

Αραμπάς περνά, αραμπάς περνά,
ωχ μανούλα μου, η καρδιά μου πως κτυπάει!
Η σατράπισσα που αγάπησα με άλλον πάει.

ΠΑΛΙΩΣΕ ΤΟ ΣΑΚΑΚΙ ΜΟΥ

Πάλιωσε το σακάκι μου,
θα σβήσω απ' το μεράκι μου,

Here's to you brave lads, good luck to you,
here's to you brave lads who bring us sponges,
black coral and pearls, from the shore.

Syrtos. Bayaderas. Recorded in 1947 with Stellakis and Ioanna Yiorgakopoulou.

WHEN YOU DRINK IN THE TAVERN

When you drink in the tavern, you sit without speaking,
you sigh now and then from the depths of your heart.

I'd like to ask you and find out for myself
what sorrow it is that makes you so sad?

Maybe you loved and got cheated too.
Come, sit down with us — we'll have some fun together.

Hasapiko. Tsitsanis. Recorded in 1947 with Bellou and the composer singing.

SHREW (The Carriage goes by)

The carriage goes by, the carriage goes by,
and the shrew I loved is inside.
She's in someone's arms and doesn't care, the tramp!

The carriage goes by, the carriage goes by,
with that slut who I ruined my life for.
She left me broke and busted up my home.

The carriage goes by, the carriage goes by,
ah, mother, how my heart beats!
The shrew I loved is with someone else.

Hasapiko. Tsitsanis. Two versions recorded simultaneously in 1948, one with Keromitis, Bellou and Stellakis, and the other with the composer, Soula Kalfopoulou, and Markos.

MY JACKET'S WORN OUT

My jacket's worn out,
my blues will kill me.

151

και καημό, και καημό έχω μεγάλο
δεν μπορώ, δεν μπορώ να πάρω άλλο.

Πόσα κουστούμια χάρησα;
Μα τώρα που ρεστάρησα
φίλος δε, φίλος δεν με πλησιάζει,
τα παλιά, τα παλιόρουχο κοιτάζει.

Ντυμένο σε προσέχουνε
κι' όλοι κοντά σου τρέχουνε.
Σαν παλιώ, σαν παλιώσουν περ' ως πέρα
δεν σου λέ, δεν σου λένε καλημέρα.

ΑΝΟΙΞΕ ΓΙΑΤΙ ΔΕΝ ΑΝΤΕΧΩ

Το παράθυρο κλεισμένο, σφαλισμένο, σκοτεινό.
Για ποιο λόγο δεν ανοίγεις, πεισματάρα, να σε δω;
Άνοιξε, άνοιξε, γιατί δεν αντέχω,
φτάνει πια να με τυρανάς.

Ξεροστάλιασα στ' αγιάζι, ώρες να σου τραγουδώ.
Η καρδιά μου φλόγες βγάζει, μα δεν βγαίνεις να σε δω.

Άνοιξε, άνοιξε, γιατί δεν αντέχω,
φτάνει πια να με τυρανάς.

ΨΙΛΟ ΓΑΖΙ

Με τους καυγάδες στήσαμε κι' οι δυο ψιλό γαζί,
τη γκρίνια που αρχίσαμε, δεν ξέρω τι θα βγάλει.
Σαν πέφτει γκριν' ανάμεσα, ο έρωτας δεν ζει,
το φταις και φταίω, θα μας φάει το κεφάλι.

Κακό βιολί αρχίσαμε, βρε μάγισσα, που λες,
τον τσακωμό τον πήραμε θαρρώ σκοινί γαϊτάνι.
Το καβγαδάκι π' άρχισε κι' οι γκρίνιες μας αυτές,
που να το βρεις, σε τι μπελάδες θα μας βάλει.

My pain, my pain's so bad
I can't take it, can't take any more.

How many suits did I give away?
But now that I'm flat broke
not a friend, not a friend comes near me,
he sees my old, old clothes.

When you're well-dressed
they all come running.
When your clothes wear out, wear out,
from then on they stop saying hello.

Zebekiko. Tsitsanis. Recorded in 1948 with Stella Haskil.

OPEN UP, I CAN'T BEAR IT

The window closed, bolted, dark.
Stubborn girl, why don't you open up so I can see you?

Open up, open up, I can't bear it any more,
you've tormented me for long enough.

I've waited in the frost, singing to you for hours.
My heart's on fire, but you don't come out.

Open up, open up, I can't bear it any more,
you've tormented me for long enough.

Zebekiko. Papaioannou. Recorded with Bellou and Stellakis in 1948.

ENTANGLED

We've got tangled up with all our quarrels,
this whining we've started, where will it end?
Once quarrelling starts, love doesn't last,
it's your fault, it's mine, it'll finish us off.

Mangas woman, we're caught in a rut,
this fighting will lead us round in circles.
The squabbles that start and all our nagging,
who knows in what a mess they'll land us?

153

Η φαγωμάρα μας αυτή δεν έχει τελειωμό,
ούτε κι' η γκρίνια μας ποτέ θα φτάσει σε μιαν άκρη.
Ίσως μας φέρει, όπως πάει στερνά το χωρισμό,
και να μας πνίξει και τους δυο στο μαύρο δάκρυ.

ΠΡΙΝ ΤΟ ΧΑΡΑΜΑ

Πριν το χάραμα μονάχος εξεκίνησα
και στο πρώτο μας το στέκι την αυγούλα γύρισα.
Πριν ακόμα σβήσουν τ' άστρα εξεπόρτισα
να ξανάβρω τα δυο σου χείλη που ποτέ δεν χόρτασα.
Αν και άλλη μ' είχε μπλέξει με καμώματα,
σ' αγαπώ κι' ήρθα κοντά σου πριν τα ξημερώματα.

ΣΚΟΤΕΙΝΙΑΣΕ

Σκοτείνιασε, σκοτείνιασε, και ερήμωσαν της Αθήνας τα στενά,
σκοτείνιασε και εγώ μόνος περπατώ στα σκοτεινά.
Ίσως κανείς να ξέρει τον καημό μου
κι' όποιος με δει ευθύς θα πει πως είμαι το παιδί του δρόμου.

Δυστύχησα, δυστύχησα, και με δέρνουν τώρα όλοι οι καιροί,
δυστύχησα και μου' καναν τη ζωή πικρή.
Ως και αυτή η μοίρα μου με κατατρέχει,
όπου σταθώ κι' όπου βρεθώ ή θα χιονίζει ή θα βρέχει.

Σκοτείνιασε, σκοτείνιασε, το κορμί μου θέλει να ξεκουραστεί.
Σκοτείνιασε, ας πεθάνω κάποια νύχτα σαν κι' αυτή,
όποιος μπορεί να με πάρει να με θάψει,
είμαι του δρόμου το παιδί, κι' αυτός μονάχα ας με κλάψει.

There's no way out of all our fighting,
this nagging's never going to end.
The way it's going, maybe we'll part,
then we'll both drown in bitter tears.

Zebekiko. Dimitrios Semsis and Manolis Hiotis, 1946.

BEFORE DAYBREAK

Before daybreak I set out alone
and went to our old haunt at dawn.

I left before the stars had faded
to find those lips I never tired of.

And if I got caught by another girl's fancy tricks,
I love you and came to you before dawn.

Zebekiko. Papaioannou. Recorded in 1948 with Odysseas Moskhonas and Stellakis.

DARKNESS HAS FALLEN

Darkness has fallen and the narrow streets of Athens are deserted,
darkness has fallen and I walk alone in the gloom.
Perhaps no one knows my sadness
and whoever sees me will say straight away I'm a street boy.

I was unlucky, I was unlucky, and now I suffer wind and cold,
I was unlucky and my life became bitter.
Now fate pursues me everywhere,
wherever I go it rains or snows.

Darkness has fallen and my body wants to rest.
Darkness has fallen; if I'm to die on a night like this,
whoever is about can take me and bury me,
I'm a boy of the street, and only it will weep for me.

Hasapiko. Yiorgos Mitsakis, 1949.

ΤΡΕΛΗ, ΠΟΥ ΘΕΛΕΙΣ ΝΑ ΜΕ ΣΤΕΦΑΝΩΣΕΙΣ

Τρελή, που θέλεις να με στεφανώσεις
και νύφη στο πλευρό μου να σταθείς.
Μα ξέρεις πως πικρά θα μετανιώσεις
και γρήγορα στους δρόμους θα βρεθείς.

Δεν κάνω εγώ για γάμο και για σπίτι,
κουράζομαι στα ίδια τα φιλιά.
Γουστάρω να γυρνώ σαν το σπουργίτι
κι' όπου βρεθώ να κτίζω τη φωλιά.

Παντρέψου κάναν άλλο νοικοκύρη
και πνίξε της καρδιάς σου τον καημό.
Μ' εμένα το ρεμπέτη και μπατίρη
στα σίγουρα θα πέσεις στο γκρεμό.

ΝΥΧΤΕΣ ΞΕΝΥΧΤΩ

Νύχτες ξενυχτώ χωρίς ελπίδα,
έρημος στους δρόμους τριγυρίζω.
Μπρος στο παράθυρό σου στη γρίλια
τις θλιμμένες ώρες μου περνάω.

Πόσο νοσταλγώ να σ' ανταμώσω,
να ξανάβρω την παλιά χαρά,
τα φιλιά μου πάλι να σου δώσω,
να μου φύγει η μαύρη συμφορά.

Μα εκεί που βρίσκεσαι στα ξένα,
ποιος να ξέρει τώρα που γυρνάς;
Άραγε με σκέφτεσαι κι' εμένα
ή για κάποιον άλλονε πονάς.

CRAZY GIRL, YOU WANT TO MARRY ME

Crazy girl, you want to marry me
and stand beside me as a bride.
You'd better know you'd soon regret it
and find yourself on the streets again.

I'm not the type to settle down,
I soon get bored with the same kisses.
I love to wander like a sparrow
and build my nest where I happen to be.

Go marry some other house-proud fellow
and drown the sorrows in your heart.
With a man like me, a rembetis who's broke,
it's quite certain you'll come to grief.

Hasapiko. Tsitsanis. First recorded in 1949.

NIGHTS I STAY AWAKE

Nights I stay awake without hope,
lonely, I walk the streets.
In front of the bars of your window
I spend my sad hours.

How I long to meet you again,
to find our old joy once more,
to give you again my kisses
so my black sadness will leave.

But there, in some strange land,
who knows where you wander now?
I wonder if you think of me
or suffer for someone else.

Hasapiko. Papaioannou, 1950.

OI ΦΑΜΠΡΙΚΕΣ

Σφυρίζ' η φάμπρικα μόλις χαράζει,
οι εργάτες τρέχουν για δουλειά,
για να δουλέψουν όλη την ημέρα.
Γεια σου περήφανη και αθάνατη δουλειά!

Βλέπεις κοπέλες στα υφαντουργεία
κι' άλλες δουλεύουν στ' αργαλιά,
στα καπνομάγαζα, στα συνεργεία.
Γεια σου περήφανη και αθάνατη δουλειά!

Φράγκο δεν δίνουν για μεγαλεία,
έχουν μάθει να ζουν απλά,
στάζ' ο ιδρώτας τους χρυσές σταγόνες.
Γεια σου περήφανη και αθάνατη δουλειά!

Σφυρίζει η φάμπρικα σα θα σχολάσουν,
κορίτσια-αγόρια ξευγαρωτά,
με την αγάπη τους θα ξαποστάσουν.
Γεια σου περήφανη και αθάνατη εργατιά!

ΒΑΡΕΙΑ ΜΕΣΑΝΥΧΤΑ

Μες στα βαρειά μεσάνυχτα
η πόρτα μου χτυπάει,
δεν φαίνεται όμως κανείς.
Ποιος νάναι; Τι ζητάει;
Στο σπίτι αυτό τ' αραχνιασμένο
τι έχω πια να περιμένω;

Δεν έχω μάνα κι' αδερφούς
για να τους περιμένω.
Έλιωσα στο κρεβάτι μου
το Χάρο πια προσμένω,
και του τοίχου το ρολόι
αρχινά το μοιρολόι.

THE FACTORIES

The factory whistle blows at first light,
the workers hurry off to work,
labouring the whole day long.
Here's to proud, immortal labour!

See the girls in the textile mills
and others who work at the looms,
in the cigarette factories, the tool-shops.
Here's to proud, immortal labour!

They don't give a damn for worldly fame,
they've learned to live life simply,
their sweat drips in golden drops.
Here's to proud, immortal labour!

The whistle blows for them to leave,
girls and boys come out in pairs,
in their love they'll find respite.
Here's to proud, immortal labour!

Zebekiko. Tsitsanis. Recorded in 1950 with Prodromos Tsaousakis, Marika Ninou and the composer.

DEEP MIDNIGHT

In the deep midnight
there's a knock at my door
but no one appears.
Who can it be? What do they want?
In this house of cobwebs
what more can I wait for?

I've no mother or brothers
nor sisters to wait for.
Wasting on my bed
I wait for Death,
and the clock on the wall
leads the funeral dirge.

Σώσε με, Παναγίτσα μου,
τα νιάτα μου λυπήσου!
Διώξε το Χάρο απ' την αυλή
να μην τον αντικρίσω!
Και του τοίχου το ρολόι
αρχινά το μοιρολόι.

ΗΛΙΟΒΑΣΙΛΕΜΑ ΣΩΣΤΟ

Ηλιοβασίλεμα σωστό, την ώρα που νυχτώνει,
σκυφτός τραβώ το δρόμο μου, καημός με μαραζώνει.
Γκρίζα γινήκαν τα μαλλιά, λύγισε το κορμί μου,
και το μαράζι ρίζωσε βαθιά μες την ψυχή μου.
Πόνοι με δέρνουνε πολλοί, καημοί με βασανίζουν,
και κάθε μέρα που περνά τα νιάτα μου τσακίζουν.

ΠΑΙΞΤΕ ΜΠΟΥΖΟΥΚΙΑ!

Πόσο βασανίστηκα κοντά σου!
Πόσο πλήρωσα την απονιά σου!
Κακούργα, εσύ μου τόκλεισες το σπίτι,
και τώρα χαίρεσαι που μ' έκανες αλήτη.

Παίξτε μπουζούκι! παίξτε βιολιά!
μια πονεμένη ψυχή το ζητά.
Παίξτε απόψε να σπάσει, παιδιά,
του αλήτη η καρδιά.

Τη ζωή μου έπαιξα με σένα,
τη ζημιά σου πλήρωσα με αίμα.
Ότι είχα σε μια νύχτα τόχω χάσει
γιατί στη μαύρη σου ψυχή έδωσα βάση.

Δυο καρδιές αφήνεις μες το κλάμα·
πόνεσε η δόλια μου η μάνα

Save me, Virgin,
pity my youth!
Drive Death from my yard
so I won't have to meet him!
And the clock on the wall
leads the funeral dirge.

Zebekiko. Takis Lavidas. Recorded, ca. 1950, with Bellou.

TRUE SUNSET

True sunset, the hour when night falls,
I make my way stooping, broken by sorrow.

My hair's turned grey, my body's bent,
the sadness has taken deep roots in my soul.

Pain lashes me, sorrow torments me,
and each day that passes destroys my youth.

Zebekiko. Yiorgos Lafkas. Recorded by Kreouzis and Ioanna Yiorgakopoulou, ca. 1951.

PLAY BOUZOUKIS!

What I've suffered, being near you!
How I've paid for your heartlessness!
You've cost me my house, you evil bitch,
and now you're pleased you've made me a bum.

Play bouzoukis! play violins!
an aching heart is begging you.
Play tonight, boys, until it breaks
the heart of a poor vagabond.

I played my whole life out with you
and paid in blood for the trouble you caused.
I lost all I had in one night for you
because I trusted your black heart.

Two hearts you're leaving in tears:
my poor mother suffered who raised me

που με μεγάλωσε με πίκρες, με νυχτέρια,
για να με πνίξουν τα μαύρα σου τα χέρια.

ΦΤΩΧΟΠΑΙΔΟ

Φτωχόπαιδο με γνωρίζεις,
κι' από μικρό στην πιάτσα
παλεύω με τα μπράτσα,
στα σίδερα, στα γράσα,
κι' όπου νυχτώσω και βρεθώ.

Κι' αν κάθε βράδυ ξενυχτώ
στη ρόδα, στο τιμόνι,
και μην παραπονιέσαι
και μην στεναχωριέσαι
που μένεις πάντα μοναχή.

Σ' αυτή τη δύσκολη ζωή
θέλει πολλά στραπάτσα.
Γι' αυτό κι' εγώ στην πιάτσα
παλεύω με τα γράσα
για σένα, αγάπη μου γλυκιά.

ΟΙ ΒΑΛΙΤΣΕΣ

Δεν το περίμενα ποτέ
να φύγεις, να μ' αφήσεις,
να πάρεις τις βαλίτσες σου
κι' αλλού να πάς να ζήσεις.

Κι' αν μετανιώσεις μη φοβηθείς
κοντά μου να γυρίσεις.

Δεν σε μισώ κι' αν μου 'φυγες,
και βάλτο στο μυαλό σου,
αχάριστα κι' αν φέρθηκες,
δεν θέλω το κακό σου.

with bitterness, working night shifts,
only to see your black hands choke me.

Hasapiko. Tsitsanis. Recorded in 1953 with Mairi Linda.

POOR BOY

You know I'm a poor boy,
and since I was a kid here
I've worked with my hands
in the iron and grease,
and I sleep where I can.

If I stay up every night
at the wheel, at the helm,
don't complain, girl,
and don't be sad
that you're left alone.

In this hard life
you need lots of guts.
That's why I struggle
alone in the grease
for you, sweet love.

Zebekiko. Tsitsanis. Recorded in 1953 with the composer and Marika Ninou singing.

THE SUITCASES

I never thought I'd see the day
you'd go away and leave me,
that you'd pack up your suitcases
and leave for somewhere else.

And if you regret it, don't be afraid
to come right back to me.

I don't hate you although you left me,
and get it into your head,
even if you treated me wrong,
I don't wish you any harm.

Το μονοπάτι που τραβάς
αν θα βγεις γελασμένη,
θυμήσου μια φτωχή καρδιά
που πάντα σε προσμένει.

ΓΙΑΝΝΗ

Βρε, καλώς τόνε το Γιάννη,
που μας έφερε βοτάνι.
Δεν κονόμησα, να πούμε,
το βοτάνι για να πιούμε.
Πάρε λίρες κι' άντε βρέστο,
βαρύ πλήρωστο και φέρτο.
Μες το πόστο στη μαγκιά
δεν υπάρχει ούτε ουγκιά.
Φέρε, Γιάννη, το βοτάνι
την ψυχή μας για να γιάνει.

ΤΑ ΜΑΤΟΚΛΑΔΑ ΣΟΥ ΛΑΜΠΟΥΝ

Τα ματόκλαδά σου λάμπουν, βρε!
σαν τα λούλουδα του κάμπου.
Τα ματόκλαδά σου γέρνεις, βρε!
νου και λογισμό μου παίρνεις.
Τα ματάκια σ' αδερφούλα, βρε!
μου ραγίζουν την καρδούλα.
Τα ματάκια σου να βγούνε, βρε!
σαν και μένα δεν θα βρούνε.

On the lonely path you've chosen
if life makes a fool of you,
remember a poor heart
that will always be waiting for you.

Zebekiko. Papaioannou, early 1950s. This was the first song Stelios Kazantzides recorded.

YIANNI

It's good to see you, Yianni,
you've brought us weed to smoke.

I didn't score, let's say, any weed
for us to smoke.

Take some cash and find it,
pay a fortune and bring it.

There isn't an ounce to be had
in all the usual hang-outs.

Yianni, bring on the weed
and give our souls some peace.

Zebekiko. Haralambos Maltezos (Pagoni, Aegina). The song is written in the form of a dialogue; it has never been recorded.

YOUR EYELASHES SHINE

Your eyelashes shine, oh!
like the flowers of the field.

You lower your eyelashes, oh!
and blow my mind away!

Your eyes, little sister, oh!
break my heart in two.

And when your eyes open, oh!
they won't find another like me.

Zebekiko. Markos. Recorded 1960. Possibly based on an older song.

9

Autographs

ΑΛΗΤΗΣ

Αλήτη μ' είπες μια βραδιά χωρίς καμιά αιτία,
μα του αλήτη η καρδιά δεν σου κρατάει κακία.

Αλήτη μ' είπες, μα εγώ αντί να σε μισήσω,
γελώ ακόμα κι' αν πονώ για να μη σε λυπήσω.

Θα 'ρθει καιρός όμως, μικρή, να το μετανοήσεις,
για του αλήτη την καρδιά θα κλάψεις, θα δακρύσεις.

BUM

You called me a bum one evening without any reason,
but the bum's heart doesn't hold it against you.

You called me a bum, but instead of hating you
I laugh even if it hurts, so that I won't make you sad.

There'll come a time, though, when you'll regret it, little girl,
when you'll cry and you'll weep for the heart of a bum.

Zebekiko. Hadzichristos, 1938; words, Lelakis.

Lelakis

ΑΛΗΤΗΣ

Αλήτη μ' είπες μια βραδιά
χωρίς καρδιά ...
μα του Αλήτη η καρδιά
δεν σου ...

Αλήτη μ' είπες· μα εγώ
αντί να σε μισήσω
... μια ...
για να μη σε ...

θάρθη καιρός όμως ...
να το ...
του Αλήτη την καρδιά
...

Ιωάννης Κ. Λελάκης
Δραγατσάνια 1938

ΣΥΝΝΕΦΙΑΣΜΕΝΗ ΚΥΡΙΑΚΗ

Συννεφιασμένη Κυριακή,
μοιάζεις με την καρδιά μου
που έχει, που έχει πάντα συννεφιά,
Χριστέ και Παναγιά μου.

Είσαι μια μέρα σαν κι' αυτή
που 'χασα τη χαρά μου,
συννεφιασμένη Κυριακή,
ματώνεις την καρδιά μου.

Όταν σε βλέπω βροχερή
στιγμή δεν ησυχάζω,
μαύρη μου κάνεις τη ζωή
και βαριαναστενάζω.

CLOUDY SUNDAY

Cloudy Sunday,
you look like my heart
which is always cloudy,
Christ and the Virgin.

You're a day like the one
when I lost my joy;
cloudy Sunday,
you make my heart bleed.

When I see you rainy
I can't find a moment's peace;
you make my life black
and I sigh deeply.

Zebekiko. Tsitsanis, 1943–4. First recorded in 1948 with Tsaousakis and Bellou.

Tsitsanis

Συννεφιασμένη Κυριακή
μοιάζεις με την καρδιά μου
που έχει πάντα συννεφιά
Χριστέ και Παναγιά μου.

Σαν μια μέρα σαν και σένα
μου χάθηκε η χαρά μου,
συννεφιασμένη Κυριακή
ματώνεις την καρδιά μου.

Όταν σε βλέπω βροχερή
στιγμή δεν ησυχάζω
μαύρη μου κάνεις τη ζωή
και βαριαναστενάζω.

Β. Τσιτσάνης

ΠΕΡΑΣΜΕΝΑ ΞΕΧΑΣΜΕΝΑ

Καθημερινώς με τυραννάς
μα εσύ για άλλονε πονάς.
Ή εμένα ν' αγαπήσεις
ή να φύγεις να μ' αφήσεις.

Μα σαν και μένα δεν θα βρεις.
Άκου και μένα να χαροίς!
Έλα να τα ξαναπούμε
μια και θες να χωριστούμε.

Θα 'ρθοι στιγμή να θυμηθης,
μα όσα πλούτη και να βρης
τότε θαναι πια για μένα
περασμένα ξεχασμένα.

Περασμένα ξεχασμένα,
κι απ' την καρδιά σβησμένα.

PAST, FORGOTTEN

You torment me every day
but you suffer for someone else.
Either love me
or go away and leave me.

You won't find another like me.
Listen to me and you'll be happy!
Come and let's talk it over,
now you want to separate.

There'll come a moment when you'll remember,
but however rich a man you find
you'll be, for me,
past, forgotten.

Past, forgotten,
and wiped out of my heart.

Hasaposerviko. Moskhonas, 1946.

Moskhonas

ΠΕΡΑΣΜΕΝΑ ΞΕΧΑΣΜΕΝΑ

ΚΑΘΗΜΕΡΙΝΩΣ ΜΕ ΤΗΡΑΝΝΑΣ
ΜΑ ΕΣΗ ΓΙΑ ΑΛΛΟΝΕ ΠΟΝΑΣ
Η ΕΜΕΝΑ Ν ΑΓΑΠΗΣΙΕΣ
Η ΝΑ ΦΗΓΕΙΣ ΝΑ Μ ΑΦΗΣΕΙΣ

ΓΙΑ ΣΑΝ ΚΙ ΕΜΕΝΑ ΔΕΝΘΑΒΡΕΙ
ΑΚΟΥ ΚΑΙ ΜΕΝΑ ΝΑ ΧΑΡΟΙΣ
ΕΛΑ ΝΑ ΤΑ ΞΑΝΑΠΟΥΜΕ
ΜΙΑ ΚΑΙ ΘΕΣ ΝΑ ΧΩΡΙΣΤΟΥ

ΘΑΡΘΟΙ ΣΤΙΓΜΗ ΝΑ ΘΗΜΗΘΗΣ
ΜΑ ΟΣΑ ΠΛΟΥΤΗ ΚΑΙ ΝΑ ΒΡΗΣ
ΤΟΤΕ ΘΑΝΑΙ ΠΙΑ ΓΙΑ ΜΕΝΑ
ΠΕΡΑΣΜΕΝΑ
ΠΕΡΑΣΜΕΝΑ ΞΕΧΑΣΜΕΝΑ
Κ ΑΠ ΤΗΝ ΚΑΡΔΙΑ ΣΒΗΣΜΕΝΑ
ΧΑΣΑΠΟΣΕΡΒΙ79 46
ΟΟυ κο ΜΟΣΧΟΝΑΣ

171

Η ΑΤΑΧΤΗ

Ήθελα να σ' αντάμωνα,
να σου 'λεγα καμπόσα,
κι αν δεν σου γύριζα το νου
να μου 'κοβαν τη γλώσα.

Δεν σε θέλω, δεν σε θέλω, πια δεν σ' αγαπώ·
δεν σε θέλω, πάρε δρόμο κι άντε στο καλό.

Μου το 'πανε η μάγισσα
κι όλες οι καφετζούδες,
μου το 'πε μια απ' την Αίγυπτο
με τις φαρδιές πλεξούδες.

Και τι δεν έκανα για σε
για να σε διορθώσω,
μα συ τόσο άταχτη
στρίψε για να γλιτώσω!

MISBEHAVER

I've been wanting to meet you,
to tell you a thing or two,
and if I don't get it into your head
they can cut my tongue right out.

I don't want you, I don't want you, I don't love you any more;
I don't want you, hit the road and here's good luck to you!

The witch told me this
and the women who read coffee cups,
an Egyptian woman told me
whose braids were long and thick.

And what didn't I do for you
to try to straighten you out,
but you're so incorrigible,
beat it and give me a break!

Zebekiko. Markos. First recorded in 1965(?).

Markos

Η ΑΤΑΧΤΗ

Ηθελα να σαν λα γονα
να σον λε γα Καμποσα
Κιαρ δε σον ιριγα το Νου
Ναμον Κοβαν ιπ γλοσα

ρ γ ριν
Δεν σε θε γο Δεν σε θε γο
Πιω δεν σα γι ωο δεν σε θε γο
Παρε δρο γιο κιαιγε δλο κα γο

Μουλουωανε Η Μαγιος
Κιολσι Η Καγιγουδες
Νου γο Μιω αωθιν Αιριωγο
Με ιπι γαρδις Πελε γουδες

Και ιπ δεν ειανα ιιανε
ιια να σι διορθοσο
Μαγιω γοοο Αγαχιπ
Θριπσι ιιανα γλι ιοοο

Μαρκος Βαρβαιμρχ

Papazoglou

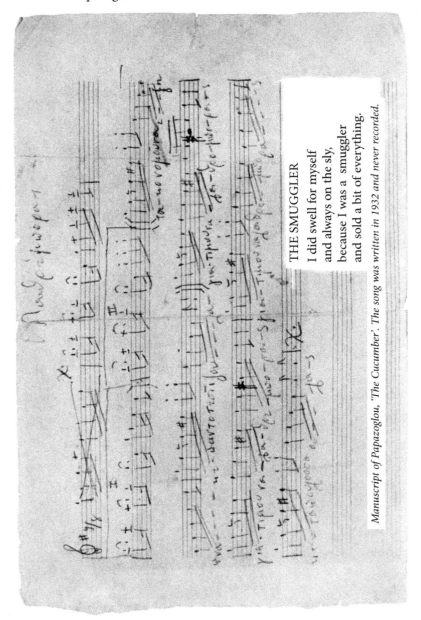

THE SMUGGLER

I did swell for myself
and always on the sly,
because I was a smuggler
and sold a bit of everything.

Manuscript of Papazoglou, 'The Cucumber'. The song was written in 1932 and never recorded.

Bibliography

There are now many publications on the rembetika, most of them in Greek, and for those who read Greek I refer them to Κώστας Βλησίδης, *Για μια Βιβλιογραφία του Ρεμπέτικου 1873-2001* (Athens: Εκδόσεις του Εικοστού Πρώτου, 2002), which provides an exhaustive bibliography of articles and books not only in Greek but also in other languages. For those who wish to read further in English, in addition to the publications that are referred to in the text I list below other sources that have been published in English.

Einarsson, Mats. 'Some aspects of form as an intersubjective frame-work in instrumental improvisations (*taximia*) in Greek bouzou-ki music', in *Proceedings of the 2nd British-Swedish Conference on Musicology: Ethnomusicology*, Cambridge, 1989, pp. 181–95.

Fatouras, A. 'Night without Moon', *Journal of the Hellenic Diaspora*, vol. 3, no. 4, 1976, pp. 17–28.

Frangos, Steve. 'The Last Café-Aman Performer', *Journal of Modern Hellenism*, 12–13, 1995–6, pp. 239–57.

Gauntlett, Stathis. *Rebetika Carmina Graeciae Recentioris — A contri-bution to the definition of the term and the genre* Rebetiko Tragoudi *through a detailed analysis of its verses and of the evolu-tion of its performance*. Athens: Denise Harvey, 1985.

——. 'Orpheus in the Criminal Underworld. Myth in and about Rebetika', *Mantatophoros*, 34, 1989, pp. 7–48.

——. 'Folklore and Populism: The "Greening" of the Greek Blues', in Margaret Clarke (ed.), *Proceedings of the Fourth National Folklore Conference*. Canberra, Australia, 1991, pp. 85–91.

Holst-Warhaft, Gail. 'Resisting Translation: Slang and Subversion in the Rebetika', *Journal of Modern Greek Studies*, vol. 8, 1990, pp. 183–96.

——. 'Rebetika, the Double-Descended Deep Songs of Greece', in William Washabaugh (ed.), *The Passion of Music and Dance: Body, Gender and Sexuality*. Oxford: Berg, 1998, pp. 111–26.

——. Sections on music and dance in Stratos Constantinides (ed.), *Greece in Modern Times: An Annotated Bibliography of Works published in English in Twenty-Two Academic Disciplines during the Twentieth Century*. Lanham, MD: Scarecrow Press, 2000, pp. 241–50.

——. 'Re-orienting the Rebetika', *Musica e storia*. University of Bologna, 2002, pp. 547–69.

——. 'The Female Dervish and Other Shady Ladies of the Rebetika', in Tullia Magrini (ed.), *Music and Gender: Perspectives from the Mediterranean*. University of Chicago Press, 2002, 169–94.

——. 'The Tame Sow and the Wild Boor: Hybridization and the Rebetika', in Gerhard Steingress (ed.), *Songs of the Minotaur: Hybridization and popular music in the age of globalization: a comparative analysis of rebetika, tango, rai, flamenco, sardana and English urban folk*. Munster: Lit Verlag, 2002, 21–50.

Hunt, Yvonne. *Traditional Dance in Greek Culture*. Athens: Centre for Asia Minor Studies, 1996, pp. 143–8.

Kaloyanides, Michael. 'New York and the Bouzoukia: The Rise of Greek-American Music', in *Essays in Arts and Sciences*, vol. 6/1, 1977, pp. 95–103.

Manuel, Peter. 'Rebetika', in *Popular Music of the Non-Western World*. Oxford University Press, 1988, pp. 127–36.

Michael, Despina. 'Tsitsanis and the Birth of the "New" Laïko Tragoudi', *Modern Greek Studies* (Australia and New Zealand), vol. 4, 1996, pp. 55–96.

Monos, Dimitri. 'Rebetiko: The Music of the Greek Urban Working Class', *International Journal of Politics, Culture and Society*, vol. 1–2, 1987, pp. 111–19.

Pennanen, Risto Pekka. 'The Nationalization of Ottoman Popular Music in Greece', *Ethnomusicology*, vol. 48, 1, 2004, pp. 1–25.

——. 'The Development of Chordal Harmony in Greek Rebetika and Laïka Music, 1930s to 1960s', *British Journal of Ethnomusicology*, vol. 6, 1997, pp. 65–116.

Petropoulos, Ilias, trans. Ed Emory. *Songs of the Greek Underworld: The Rebetika Tradition.* London: Saqi Books, 2000. (English translation of the introduction and some song texts from Petropoulos's *Ρεμπέτικα Τραγούδια,* which was published by the author in Athens, 1968. An expanded Greek edition with many more photographs and new illustrations by A. Fassianos was published by Kedros, Athens, in 1992.)

Smith, Ole. 'Research on Rebetika: Some Methodological Problems and Issues', *Journal of Modern Hellenism*, 6, 1989, pp. 177–90.

——. 'Rebetika in the United States before World War II', in Dan Georgakas and Charles Moskos (eds.), *New Directions in Greek American Studies.* New York: Pella, 1991, pp. 318–24.

——. 'The Chronology of Rebetiko: A Reconsideration of the Evidence', *Byzantine and Modern Greek Studies*, vol. 15, 1991, pp. 318–24.

——. 'Cultural Identity and Cultural Interaction: Greek music in the United States, 1917–1941', *Journal of Modern Greek Studies*, vol. 13, 1995, pp. 125–35.

Spires, William. 'The Bouzouki. Its Evolution: a Modern Transformation', *Frets*, vol. 7/3, 1985, pp. 24–9.

Spottswood, Richard. *Ethnic Music on Record. A Discography of Ethnic Recordings Produced in the United States, 1893–1942.* Urbana and Chicago: University of Illinois, 1990.

Steingress, Gerhard. 'Social Theory and the Comparative History of Flamenco, Tango, and Rebetika', in William Washabaugh (ed.), *The Passion of Music and Dance: Body, Gender and Sexuality.* Oxford: Berg, 1998, pp. 151–7.

Strötbaum, Hugo. 'Seventy-eight Revolutions Per Minute in the Levant.' Utrecht Turcological Series, III, 1992, pp. 149–88.

Torp, Lisbet. *Salonikios — 'The Best Violin in the Balkans'.* Copenhagen: Museum Tusculanum Press, 1993.

——. 'An Urban Milieu and its Means of Expression: A Case Study of the Rebetika', in A. Buckley, K. Edstrom and P. Nixon (eds.),

Proceedings of the 2nd British-Swedish Conference on Musicology: Ethnomusicology, 1989. Göthenberg, 1991, pp. 371–80.

Tsounis, Demeter. 'Kefi and Meraki in Rebetika Music of Adelaide: Cultural Constructions of Passion and Expression and their Link with the Homeland', *Yearbook of Traditional Music*, vol. 27, 1995, pp. 90–103.

——. 'Metaphors of Center and Periphery in the Symbolic-Ideological Narratives of Rebetika Music-Making in Adelaide', *Modern Greek Studies* (Australia and New Zealand), vol. 3, 1995, pp. 151–74.

Selected discography

So many recordings of rembetika music are now available in Greece and other countries that it is difficult to keep pace with them. The limited selection below includes some of the excellent CDs recently produced in the UK and the US. Several web-sites now offer information about rembetika. The most comprehensive of these is the Greek site www.rebetiko.gr which has thousands of lyrics and musical examples and exhaustive discographies listed by artist, as well as an archive of photographs. On a smaller scale is the travel writer Mike Barrett's www.greektravel.com/music/rebetiko which has a nice enthusiastic introduction with a listing of his favourite CDs and free musical downloads. I have not included in my selection the many recordings of rembetika by well-known popular artists such as George Dalaras, Glykeria, Eleftheria Arvanitaki, Sophia Papazoglou and Haris Alexiou, and by the many rembetika-revival groups performing in countries all over the world. This is not for reasons of purism. Many of these artists are superb singers and musicians, and not all of them are known outside Greece. Others are scarcely known in Greece but have made a name for themselves in the US, Australia, or Scandinavia. A good example is Grigoris Maninakis, arguably the best interpreter of rembetika in the US, whose CD 'The Bomb' ('I Vomva') contains a number of amusing early songs in 'gringlish'.

Anthologies and series

Authentic Rebetica Recordings from the USA, No. 2 & 3 (Lyra, Greece).
   Many of the artists on these recordings are in fact musicians based in Greece.

179

The Greek Archives (FM Records, Greece). Each title of this series of over twenty collections is devoted to a theme or particular artist. Compiled by the rembetika pioneer Panayiotis Kounadis, this is an excellent series, although the notes in English are minimal.

Greek-Oriental Rebetica: Songs and Dances in the Asia Minor Style (Arhoolie-Folklyric, US). The quality of the original recordings from the collection of Martin Schwartz and the notes in English accompanying this CD are excellent. It includes a splendid example of an amané sung by Rita Abatzi.

Historic Urban Folk Songs from Greece (Rounder, US/Direct Distribution, UK). The songs on this compilation are mostly from the 1930s.

A History of Rembetika (Rembetiki Istoria) (Minos-EMI, Greece). This six-volume series was the first series of early rembetika reissued on LP records in the 1970s, and is still worth purchasing.

Lost Homelands: The Smyrneic Song in Greece, 1928–35 (Heritage, UK). This is one of a series of which this is the only CD currently available. The sound quality is exceptional and the notes are good.

Mortika: Rare Vintage Recordings from a Greek Underworld (Arko Records, Sweden). A carefully assembled collection of re-mastered recordings, many of them from the US with copious notes in English, translations of the lyrics, and information on matrix and catalogue numbers. Includes rare recordings from the US by Yiorgos Katsaros, Ioannis Halikias (also known as Jack Gregory), Sotiris Gavalas and Andonis Dalgas.

Mourmourika: Songs of the Greek Underworld, 1930–55 (Rounder, US/Direct Distribution, UK). Songs of the *mourmouridhes* or tough guys, the lyrics generally deal with underworld themes. The CD includes some rare songs by lesser-known artists. The sound quality is exceptional and Charles Howard's notes, transliterations and translations are a great help to the non-Greek speaker.

Rebetika: Songs of the Greek Underground, 1925–1947 (Trikont, Germany). A 2-CD set with notes in German. The collection is large and comprehensive.

Remembrances of a Musical Scene: The Smyrneiko Era (Mnimes: I mousiki skini tou smyrnaikou tragoudhiou 1907–1939, Lyra, Greece). A lavish boxed set complete with notes, translations and picture postcards of Smyrna, the CDs are arranged by the place of origin — Smyrna, Athens and New York — and contain some rare recordings of artists like Kyria Koula, the first singer among the Greek immigrants to record in the US, and by Konstantinos ('Gus') Doussas.

Road to Rembetika CD Companion (Traditional Crossroads CD 6006. 2010. New York). An excellent selection put together especially to accompany this book.

Rough Guide to Rebetika (World Music Network, UK). This CD is another good introduction to the full range of rembetika styles and performers and includes comprehensive notes in English. The sound quality is excellent.

Women of Rembetika (Rounder, US). The accompanying notes in English to this fine collection of recordings by female singers are minimal, but there are translations and photographs to compensate.

Alphabetical listing by individual artist or group

Rita Abatzi (Minos-EMI, Greece). Part of the Arheio series, this album has Greek notes.

Rita Abatzi (Lyra, Greece). A double album, the set contains brief notes in English.

Sotiria Bellou. 40 Years Bellou (*40 hronia Bellou*, Lyra, Greece).

Sotiria Bellou, Vols 3, 4, 5 (Lyra, Greece). One of the greatest voices of the rembetika in her original recordings, most of them with Tsitsanis.

Andonis Diamantidis sings Amanédhes, Rebetika and Folk Songs (O Andonis Diamantidis tragoudhaei amanedhes, rembetika kai dhimotika) (FM Records, Greece). The notes are in Greek, but this collection features the great Asia Minor singer with the major artists of the period like Dimitrios Semsis and Spyros Peristeris.

Rosa Eskenazi: Rebetissa (Rounder, US/Direct Distribution, UK). With its English notes and wide selection of recordings with artists such as Semsis and Tomboulis, this is an excellent introduction to Rosa's art.

The Rembetika of Rosa Eskenazi (Lyra, Greece).

Marika Papagika: Greek Popular and Rebetic Music in New York 1918–29 (Alma Criolla, Berkeley, California, US). A meticulously-assembled collection of high-quality and unusual recordings by the fabled singer from Kos who made her home in New York and was generally accompanied by her husband, the cymbalum-player Kostas Papagikas. Liner notes and lyrics are provided in English.

Vangelis Papazoglou: The Smyrneic Song in Greece after 1922 (To Smyrneiko Tragoudhi stin Elladha meta to 1922, Lyra, Greece). A Smyrna refugee, Papazoglou and his wife, the blind singer Angeliki, were important figures in the early Piraeus rembetika scene. The performers include Stellakis Perpiniadis, Rosa Eskenazi, Kostas Roukounas and Rita Abatzi. The sound quality is poor.

The Famous Four from Piraeus (Tetras I Xakousti tou Pireos, Anodhos, Greece). The quartet of Markos Vamvakaris, Yiorgos Batis, Stratos Payioumdzis and Artemis (Anestis Delias), the most important group of the pre-war Piraeus scene. The notes are in Greek only.

Markos Vamvakaris: Bouzouki Pioneer, 1932–1940 (Rounder, US/ Direct Distribution, UK). Excellent sound quality, good notes and quite an unusual collection of songs.

Marika Ninou at Jimmy the Fat's (I Marika Ninou stou Tzimi tou Hondrou, Athenaeum, Greece). Marika Ninou, a refugee from the Caucusus, sang with Tsitsanis from 1948 to 1956. This live recording of Ninou performing with Tsitsanis in 1955 gives the listener some idea of her charm, although the quality of the recording is poor and there are no notes. This might be supplemented by the following recording.

Marika Ninou/Vassilis Tsitsanis: Immortal Rembetika (Athanata Rembetika, Lyra, Greece). A better quality recording with many of Tsitsanis's most famous songs.

Yiannis Papaioannou: 26 Great Hits (26 Megales Epityxies, Lyra, Greece). A collection of the best-known songs of one of the most talented and beloved song-writers of the later rembetika.

Vassilis Tsitsanis 1936–1946 (Rounder, US/Direct Distribution, UK). There are many recordings and series of Tsitsanis with various singers, and the Tsitsanis enthusiasts will not be content with a single CD, but this one has the advantage of notes in English.

Ioanna Yiorgakopoulou: I Rebetissa, Vol. 1 (Minos-EMI, Greece). Among the best albums of this great and insufficiently-known singer.

Index of first lines of songs

Index of song titles

Index

Gail Holst — musician, writer, poet and scholar — is professor in the Departments of Comparative Literature and Biological and Environmental Engineering and a member of the Graduate Field of Music at Cornell University where she is also director of the Mediterranean Studies Initiative and co-director of the Cornell Middle-Eastern and Mediterranean Music Ensemble. Her areas of particular interest are modern Greek literature and music, Greek literature from antiquity to the present, translation, water and culture, interests which began to develop after her initial visit to Greece in 1966 when she first came across rembetika music. She lived for a number of years in Greece, where she played with with the composers Mikis Theodorakis and Dionysis Savvopoulos, before going to the States. Her books include *Penelope's Confession* [poems] (2007), *The Cue for Passion: Grief and its Political Uses* (2000), *Dangerous Voices: Women's Laments and Greek Literature* (1992), *Theodorakis: Myth and Politics in Modern Greek Music* (1980), and she is co-editor of *Losing Paradise: The Water Crisis in the Mediterranean* (2010) and *The Classical Moment* (1999).

CPSIA information can be obtained
at www.ICGtesting.com
Printed in the USA
BVHW07s0841270918
528671BV00001B/249/P